■ SCHOLASTIC

Check-in
Assessments
for Differentiated
Lessons

D1566845

Troy Strayer &
Beverly Strayer

New York • Toronto • London • Auckland • Sydney **Teaching**
Mexico City • New Delhi • Hong Kong • Buenos Aires *Resources*

Dedication

Floyd and Pauline Warner believed in us, encouraged us, and taught us that education is the key to a fulfilling life. They instilled a work ethic that flows through us today, and a purity of life that is the foundation of who we are and who we will always be.

Thank you, Mom and Dad. — Bev

Thank you, Grandma and Grandpa. — Troy

Acknowledgments

We'd like to thank our friends and family for believing in us and for lending their support and words of encouragement along the way. Without their love and support this would not have been possible.

We'd also like to thank our many colleagues who have taken the initiative and risk to embrace these strategies in their classrooms and who have provided us with invaluable feedback on the lessons' effectiveness and areas in need of improvement. In particular, we'd like to thank Marie Donnelly, James Jefferis, Jared Flay, Michael Grassel, Lea Kimmel, and Amy-Jo Quiñones for taking the initiative and risk to incorporate these strategies in their classrooms.

Our administration has been supportive of us throughout our learning and growing process. We'd especially like to thank Dr. Larry Macaluso, Dr. Steven Iovino, Cindy Williams, and Kevin Peters for viewing us as leaders in our school district and allowing us to grow as professionals.

Our students continue to inspire us to further our learning and bring our best to them every day.

Lastly, a huge thank-you to Sarah Longhi, Managing Editor at Scholastic Teaching Resources, and our editor, Sarah Glasscock for the many conversations and exchanges of thought that helped transform this idea into reality.

Thank you to my mother and co-author, who has always encouraged me to be me and not allow others to bring me down. — Troy

Without the friendship and guidance of Rick LoBianco, I would not be where I am today. Thank you, Ricky, and we will always Choose Happiness.

Cover design by Jorge J. Namerow

Cover photography: boy in upper left: monkeybusiness images/Bigstock.com; girl with globe: © Joshua Hodge Photography/iStock; girl reading © Jose Girarte/iStock; boy in lower right: pkujiahe/iStock; boy with magnifying glass: © Bart Coenders/iStock

Interior design by Melinda Belter

Development Editor: Sarah Longhi

Editor: Sarah Glasscock

ISBN: 978-0-545-29682-3

Copyright © 2012 Troy Strayer & Beverly Strayer

All rights reserved.

Printed in the U.S.A.

2 3 4 5 6 7 8 9 10   40   19 18 17 16 15

CONTENTS

INTRODUCTION

"The most important single factor influencing learning is what the learner already knows."

~ FROM *EDUCATIONAL PSYCHOLOGY: A COGNITIVE VIEW* BY DAVID AUSUBEL,
JOSEPH D. NOVAK, & HELEN HANESIAN

Imagine this scenario: Friends have invited you to go to a concert by one of their favorite bands. Although you're excited about the invitation, you aren't sure you want to buy the ticket because you have no prior knowledge about the band or the genre of music they play. Our guess is that you may quickly search the Internet for information about the band or a video of them in concert. Ultimately, you'll decide whether their music fits your style and make a decision about whether to attend the concert.

Now let's apply this scenario to our students. Every day, we invite them into our classrooms without giving them relevant prior knowledge of what we're about to teach them. We then ask them to learn about a topic that we have given them neither the time nor the tools to research. When we educators fail to either activate students' prior knowledge or provide the appropriate background knowledge, we are not affording them with the greatest opportunity to experience success in the classroom.

Here's another scenario: You have just finished interviewing for your first teaching position, and now you're waiting in the lobby while the interview panel discusses your qualifications. You hope they will want to schedule a second interview. To your surprise, you wait no more than five minutes before you are called back in. To your disbelief, the panel offers you a position. You eagerly accept it and leave the building filled with anticipation and excitement. In the parking lot, you call your parents and there is no answer. You move on to your best friend, who has been in your life since elementary school. No answer. You go to your address book but even then you cannot reach a single person! Your frustration mounts because you are unable to share the events of the day with anyone and to talk over what has just happened.

It may seem unrealistic to imagine our students being as excited about summarizing their learning after a meaningful lesson as you would have been about summarizing the experience of being hired for the first time, but the need to summarize is the same. In any learning experience, our students need the opportunity to organize the new information they have learned with what they already know and to store this in their long-term memory. If they do not properly summarize a lesson, students probably will not retain the information.

Robert Marzano, Debra Pickering, and Jane Pollock (2001) have identified nine categories of instructional strategies that have a direct, positive impact on student achievement. Our book will focus on two of these: activating prior knowledge and summarizing.

 Check-in Assessments for Differentiated Lessons © 2012 by Troy Strayer & Beverly Strayer • Scholastic Teaching Resources

The Need to Activate Prior Knowledge

Before explaining why activating prior knowledge is essential to learning, it is important to first discuss the many facets of prior knowledge. We often think of prior knowledge as simply the knowledge students have of a given topic, but the term also applies to their beliefs, skills, and attitudes about that topic. Together these factors have a substantial influence on how students interpret and then assimilate incoming information with their previous experiences. The process of coordinating new information with previous experiences directly affects how students apply, remember, think about, and create new knowledge. Essentially, new knowledge is directly affected and influenced by preexisting knowledge, so it is paramount that we help students access their prior knowledge before we teach new learning.

Before new information can be stored in long-term memory, it must first form a connection with information that is already present. If students have no prior knowledge about the information you are teaching, their brains will go on a quest to make a connection. While students' brains are on this quest, they are missing vital information that you are teaching. Then, when students realize they have no prior knowledge about the topic, they once again focus on your teaching, but they are now even further behind. So we must activate students' prior knowledge or provide them with a learning experience that becomes prior knowledge.

There is vast research on prior knowledge and the effect of activating that prior knowledge on learning. It has been shown that comprehension of content material can be increased if prior knowledge is activated and new content built upon that prior knowledge. Creating an opportunity to challenge our students to call on their collective experiences is essential. Through this process, we move students from the memorization of information to meaningful learning as they begin to connect learning events (Christen & Murphy, 1991).

It is not sufficient to simply introduce strategies that activate prior knowledge at the beginning of a unit and not return to them until the beginning of the next unit. Each day needs to include an activity that will engage your students' minds with their prior learning. While some strategies in this book require more time than others to implement, all of them are an effective means of either activating students' prior knowledge or providing the necessary prior knowledge for students to be successful throughout a unit.

The Need to Summarize Learning

Summarizing, simply put, is having students put what they have heard or read into their own words by identifying the main idea and weeding out everything that is not essential. It is a learning strategy, not a teaching strategy. The process of summarization enables the learners in your classroom to construct meaning and to transfer new knowledge into their long-term memory. Summarizing entails analyzing and synthesizing information, distinguishing between essential and nonessential information, and describing that new learning in a few clear, concise sentences. When students are asked to give a summary, they have to analyze information on a deep level in order to decide what information to delete, what to substitute, and what to keep (Anderson, V., & Hidi, S., 1988–1989; Hidi & Anderson, 1986).

Does the following scenario sound familiar? The end of the period is quickly approaching, and you have a few important points to make before class ends, so you rush through the important information and assign homework. The next day, you begin class by going over the homework and reviewing the last points of your lesson from the previous day. You are disappointed to find that many students have not completed the assignment because they didn't hear you; others stare at you with confused looks because you are reviewing something they didn't learn the day before. Your frustration mounts, and your students are left to wonder what it is they are expected to learn.

What's missing from the above scenario? Summarization. Students need to summarize the day's essential learning at the end of the period. This is as important as activating their prior knowledge.

Summarization serves several purposes. First, it gives teachers valuable information on how much or little a student has learned, which is essential for planning the next lesson. The intuitive teacher looks at the summaries of a given day and decides whether to reteach the concepts or to move forward.

For students, summarization deepens the learning because they are thinking at a level that goes beyond basic comprehension. They are synthesizing, analyzing, identifying key concepts, and deleting extraneous information. The process of summarization helps students "cement" the learning; hence, they retain information over a longer period of time.

Summarization skills must be explicitly taught. This is time well spent, because these skills provide a foundation for further learning. The strategies presented in this book provide many ways for content teachers to teach the skills of summarization to every student in their classroom.

The Case for Formative Assessment

Assessing students is an ongoing part of our daily lives as teachers. Formative assessment, a process that teachers and students use during instruction, provides explicit feedback to adjust ongoing teaching and learning to improve students' achievement of intended instructional outcomes (McManus, S. 2006). If we do not actively incorporate formative assessments into our daily lessons, we cannot compile the necessary data to guide our instruction to ensure student success.

Implementing formative assessments at the beginning and end of your lessons is an integral part of the planning process for you and the learning process for the students. First, formative assessments provide specific and immediate feedback so you

Check-in Assessments for Differentiated Lessons © 2012 by Troy Strayer & Beverly Strayer • Scholastic Teaching Resources

can modify and adjust learning activities for students. This feedback also allows you to mold your teaching strategies to meet the needs of your students, while providing clear and meaningful information to them about their learning. It also promotes dialogue between you and your students about the key concepts to be learned in a given lesson. This exchange of ideas helps highlight key areas for you to target in order to close the achievement gap among your students. Formative assessments also allow you to identify a lack of knowledge among individuals and in a whole class. Once you have implemented formative assessments and identified the areas that need to be addressed, you can organize your lesson to incorporate remediation by identifying the needs of your students and grouping students with peers of similar ability. Lastly, formative assessment is not about grading; the focus is on the process of learning the information. In this way, learning is based not on the extrinsic motivation of earning a letter grade but on the intrinsic motivation of gaining knowledge about an unfamiliar topic.

The Essence of Differentiation

When we think about how to differentiate instruction in our classrooms, we begin with the following basics:

- *Content:* what a student should know, understand, and be able to do
- *Process:* activities designed to help students make sense of or take ownership of the content
- *Product:* how students demonstrate and extend what they have learned

Then, keeping these basics in mind, we need to figure out how the following elements affect differentiation:

- *Readiness:* the background knowledge that students bring to a lesson or a unit, or where they are developmentally
- *Interest:* topics that students may want to explore or that will motivate them to learn; includes interests relevant to the content area as well as outside interests
- *Learning Profile:* includes learning style (i.e., a visual, auditory, tactile, or kinesthetic learner); grouping preferences (i.e., individual, small group, or large group); and environmental preferences (i.e., lots of space or a quiet area to work in)

As teachers, we can differentiate based on any one of these factors or combination of factors (Tomlinson, 1999). See the diagram on the next page.

CONTENT/PROCESS/PRODUCT DIAGRAM

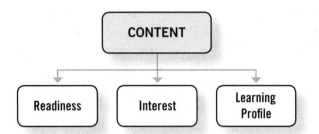

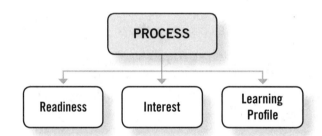

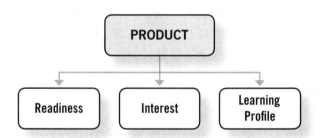

Check-in Assessments for Differentiated Lessons © 2012 by Troy Strayer & Beverly Strayer • Scholastic Teaching Resources

The chart below lists the activities, or assessment strategies, in this book, the instructional focus of each activity, and the student needs that it addresses.

ASSESSMENT STRATEGY	INSTRUCTIONAL FOCUS	STUDENT NEEDS ADDRESSED
Quick Assessments to Kick Off Lessons: Activating Prior Knowledge		
Alphabet Activator	• Content	• Readiness
Anticipation Guides	• Content • Process	• Readiness • Interest
Classroom Field Trip	• Content • Process	• Readiness • Interest • Learning Style
Cloze	• Content	• Readiness
Consensus Learning	• Content • Process	• Readiness • Learning Style
Draw What's on My Mind	• Content • Process	• Readiness • Interest • Learning Style
Entry Pass	• Content	• Readiness
Gallery Walk	• Content • Process	• Readiness • Interest • Learning Style
Make Sense of It	• Content • Process	• Readiness • Interest
Narrow It Down	• Content • Process	• Readiness • Learning Style
Sharing Ideas	• Content • Process	• Readiness • Learning Style
What Do You Know About . . . ?	• Content • Process	• Readiness • Interest
Window Pane	• Content • Process • Product	• Readiness · • Interest • Learning Style

Quick Assessments to Wrap Up Lessons: Summarizing		
Summary Frame	• Content • Process • Product	• Readiness • Interest • Learning Style
3-2-1 Blast Off!	• Content • Process • Product	• Readiness • Interest • Learning Style
Artistic Summary	• Content • Process • Product	• Readiness • Interest • Learning Style
High-Five Summary	• Content • Process • Product	• Readiness • Interest • Learning Style
Money Talks	• Content • Process • Product	• Readiness • Interest • Learning Style
Name That Word	• Content • Process • Product	• Readiness • Interest • Learning Style
Pass-Around Paragraph	• Content • Process • Product	• Readiness • Interest • Learning Style
Pass-the-Ball Summary	• Content • Process • Product	• Readiness • Interest • Learning Style
Shape-It-Up Summary	• Content • Process • Product	• Readiness • Interest • Learning Style
Incredible Shrinking Summary	• Content • Process • Product	• Readiness • Interest • Learning Style
Thinking Outside the Box	• Content • Process • Product	• Readiness • Interest • Learning Style
Throw It Out	• Content • Process • Product	• Readiness • Interest • Learning Style
You've Got Mail	• Content • Process • Product	• Readiness • Interest • Learning Style

Check-in Assessments for Differentiated Lessons © 2012 by Troy Strayer & Beverly Strayer • Scholastic Teaching Resources

How to Use This Book

You can use these lessons flexibly in your classroom. Although we have designed them to activate prior knowledge and to enhance your students' summarization skills, please use your own creativity and knowledge of your students to determine how they can best fit your content.

The 26 lessons in this book have the same format. Each lesson begins with the purpose of the strategy you will be teaching. An explanation of how the strategy helps students succeed follows in the Why It Works section. The Assessment Options section suggests alternative ways of using the strategy beyond activating prior knowledge or summarizing. To help you plan each facet of the lesson, a materials list precedes the step-by-step directions for each activity. Reproducibles and examples appear at the end of lessons.

We hope that the strategies in our book will transform learning into a personal experience for you and your students on a daily basis. When we activate students' collective experiences prior to instruction and allow them to use their own words to summarize what they've learned, they will be able to commit that learning to long-term memory, and we will foster a community of learners who memorize little but remember a lot.

Sources

Anderson, V., & Hidi, S. (1988–1989). Teaching students to summarize. *Educational Leadership, 46,* 26–28.

Ausbel, D., Novak, J. D., & Hanesian, H. (1978). Educational psychology: A cognitive view. (2nd ed.). New York: Holt, Rinehart and Winston.

Christen, W. L., & Murphy, T. J. (1991). *Increasing comprehension by activating prior knowledge.* ERIC Clearinghouse on Reading and Communication Skills, Indiana University. (ERIC No. ED328885)

Cummins, J. (2006). *Teaching strategies: Activating prior knowledge.* ESOL Online.

Hidi, S., & Anderson, V. (1986). Producing written summaries: Task demands, cognitive operations, and implications for instruction. *Review of Educational Research, 56*(4), 473–493.

Marzano, R. J., Pickering, D. J., & Pollock, J. E. (2001). *Classroom instruction that works: Research-based strategies for increasing student achievement.* Alexandria, VA: Association for Supervision and Curriculum Development.

McManus, S. (2006). Attributes of effective formative assessment. Retrieved March 20, 2009, from the Council of Chief State School Officers Web site: www.ncpublicschools.org/docs/accountability/educators/fastattributes04081.pdf.

Tomlinson, C. A. (1999). *The differentiated classroom: Responding to the needs of all learners.* Alexandria, VA: Association for Supervision and Curriculum Development.

Wormeli, R. (2004). *Summarization in any subject.* Alexandria, VA: Association for Supervision and Curriculum Development.

Quick Assessments
to Kick Off Lessons

Activating prior knowledge is like preparing the soil before sowing the seeds of knowledge.

~ JIM CUMMINS

ALPHABET ACTIVATOR

Purpose

Alphabet Activator is a strategy that allows students to demonstrate prior knowledge of a broad topic.

Why It Works

Students often enter our classrooms with more knowledge about a topic than they realize. By allowing students to demonstrate their prior knowledge about a topic, this strategy enables them to take ownership of their learning through the expression of their thoughts.

ASSESSMENT OPTIONS

Pre-Assessment

Prior to teaching a unit, give the Alphabet Activator to students to determine if the content can be compacted for the entire class. If every student has the same answer for one or more letters, you can choose to adapt the lesson(s) on that topic and go deeper than you may have previously planned. For example, if you use the Alphabet Activator for the topic of World War II, and every student writes "Holocaust" for the letter H, you can adjust how you introduce and teach your lessons on the Holocaust. If there are students who have no prior knowledge about a topic, you can partner them with students who do and then have them record several terms or phrases to activate their thinking. If you see that half your class has prior knowledge and half does not, you can group students accordingly. For the group with prior knowledge, you can provide alternative assignments to enrich their learning. For the group lacking prior knowledge, you can use more direct instruction to teach the material.

MATERIALS

Alphabet Activator reproducible for each student (page 16), pencils in different colors; materials for making and displaying a chart; notebook paper (optional)

Check-in Assessments for Differentiated Lessons © 2012 by Troy Strayer & Beverly Strayer • Scholastic Teaching Resources

Formative Assessment

Use the Alphabet Activator in the middle of a lesson or unit to gauge how students are progressing with a particular word or event. Tell students what to write beside each letter and then have them provide a brief explanation of it.

Sequence

☑ **STEP 1:** Choose a broad topic that all students have prior knowledge of, such as war, religion, science, diet, or health.

☑ **STEP 2:** Distribute an Alphabet Activator reproducible to each student.

☑ **STEP 3:** Have students draw from their prior knowledge to complete as many letter squares as they can that relate to the topic. Sample responses for the topic of World War II might be *A: atomic bomb*; *B: Berlin*; *C: Churchill*; and so on.

☑ **STEP 4:** Ask students to share their answers with a partner. If one partner has completed a letter square that the other partner left blank, have the other partner use a different-color pencil to fill in that letter square.

☑ **STEP 5:** With the whole class, brainstorm a list of possible answers and have students fill in any missing letters. Write the list on chart paper, a document camera, overhead, or an interactive whiteboard.

☑ **STEP 6:** Have students complete the summarizer at the bottom of the reproducible to show what they already knew about the topic, and new terms and phrases they learned.

Student Sample: Alphabet Activator on the topic of poetry

Name _____   Date _____

 # Alphabet Activator

Topic: _____

A	B	C	D	E
F	G	H	I	J
K	L	M	N	O
P	Q	R	S	T
U	V	W	X/Y	Z

> > > > > > > > > > > > > > > > *Summarize* ‹ ‹ ‹ ‹ ‹ ‹ ‹ ‹ ‹ ‹ ‹ ‹ ‹ ‹ ‹ ‹ ‹ ‹

What I Knew	**What I Learned**

Check-in Assessments for *Differentiated Lessons* © 2012 by Troy Strayer & Beverly Strayer • Scholastic Teaching Resources

ANTICIPATION GUIDES

Purpose

Anticipation Guides activate students' prior knowledge about a topic or provide schema for a topic that may be new to them.

Why It Works

Because students base their answers on their own beliefs and experiences, they will be required to justify their thinking either in writing or in a group discussion setting. This strategy piques student interest, sets a purpose for learning, and encourages higher-level thinking.

ASSESSMENT OPTIONS

Pre-Assessment

You may use Anticipation Guides before introducing a topic to encourage students to make predictions about its major ideas or themes.

Formative Assessment

After students have learned the content, you may also use Anticipation Guides to assess how well they understand the material and to determine whether any of their initial misconceptions have been corrected.

Anticipation Guides can be used in all content areas and with text as well as with visual media, such as video clips or films.

MATERIALS

materials to create and display Anticipation Guides (see Examples 1–4, pages 19–20)

Sequence

☑ **STEP 1:** Identify the key concepts within the lesson or unit.

☑ **STEP 2:** Predict student beliefs or experiences about the concepts that the text will either challenge or support.

☑ STEP 3: Create an Anticipation Guide for the topic. Students will record their responses in the first column. In the second column, include five to seven true/false or yes/no statements that will contest or change students' understanding of the content. Include some statements that they are sure to agree with. After you teach the lesson or unit, have students fill in the third column. They will either agree with their original thought or change it based on their learning. (See Example 1.)

☑ STEP 4: After students have completed their individual Anticipation Guide, display a revised Anticipation Guide on an interactive whiteboard or overhead display. This guide should include a new second column for student explanations. Read each statement and then ask students whether they agree or disagree with it and to explain their answer. Have multiple students share their thoughts and record the consensus answer of the group. Their explanations can be used as a pre-assessment to guide future instruction. Another option is to have students explain their answer in a small-group setting before you teach the content. (See Example 2.)

☑ STEP 5: After teaching the content, refer back to the Anticipation Guide and have students determine whether their original thoughts were correct. If not, tell students to create a new column on their Anticipation Guide and write the correct information in it. (See Example 3.)

INFERENCE VARIATION Another option for the Anticipation Guide is to include a column for making inferences about the content. Students will use what they have learned to infer what they might learn in the upcoming units. They will complete this Anticipation Guide after mastering the content, and it can assist them in predicting future topics. This will assist you in planning your lessons and will promote higher-level thinking skills in your students. (See Example 4.)

Example 1: Anticipation Guide

T/F	Statements About Andrew Jackson	T/F
	Andrew Jackson had a normal childhood.	
	Andrew Jackson was able to remain calm and keep his temper in check in tough situations.	
	Andrew Jackson gave his friends jobs in the White House.	
	Andrew Jackson favored the wealthy.	
	Andrew Jackson threatened to hang his vice president.	
	Andrew Jackson was a friend of the Native Americans.	
T	Andrew Jackson was a friend of the common people.	T

Example 2: Anticipation Guide With Answers Explained

T/F	Why I Answered This Way	Statements About Andrew Jackson	T/F
		Andrew Jackson had a normal childhood.	
F	I have seen the picture of him as a king and thought he may be a man who lost his temper easily.	Andrew Jackson was able to remain calm and keep his temper in check in tough situations.	
		Andrew Jackson gave his friends jobs in the White House.	
		Andrew Jackson favored the wealthy.	
		Andrew Jackson threatened to hang his vice president.	
		Andrew Jackson was a friend of the Native Americans.	
		Andrew Jackson was a friend of the common people.	

Example 3: Anticipation Guide With Student Corrections

T/F	Statements About Andrew Jackson	T/F	Corrections to My Original Answer
	Andrew Jackson had a normal childhood.		
	Andrew Jackson was able to remain calm and keep his temper in check in tough situations.		
F	Andrew Jackson gave his friends jobs in the White House.	T	He fired over 600 federal employees and replaced them with supporters and friends.
	Andrew Jackson favored the wealthy.		
	Andrew Jackson threatened to hang his vice president.		
	Andrew Jackson was a friend of the Native Americans.		
	Andrew Jackson was a friend of the common people.		

Example 4: Anticipation Guide With Inferences

T/F	Statements About Andrew Jackson	T/F	Inferences About What Might Happen
	Andrew Jackson had a normal childhood.		
	Andrew Jackson was able to remain calm and keep his temper in check in tough situations.		
	Andrew Jackson gave his friends jobs in the White House.		
	Andrew Jackson favored the wealthy.		
	Andrew Jackson threatened to hang his vice president.		
T	Andrew Jackson was a friend of the Native Americans.	F	Native Americans will struggle to keep their land.
	Andrew Jackson was a friend of the common people.		

Check-in Assessments for Differentiated Lessons © 2012 by Troy Strayer & Beverly Strayer • Scholastic Teaching Resources

CLASSROOM FIELD TRIP

Purpose

Classroom Field Trip provides students with knowledge about a detailed topic through movement and conversation.

Why It Works

Prior to learning about a new topic that may be unfamiliar to them, students are exposed through visuals and text to material they will learn throughout the lesson. This provides the necessary background knowledge to increase their comprehension of the topic and also retain it.

ASSESSMENT OPTION

Summative Assessment

After teaching the topic, you can have students complete a Classroom Field Trip Guide reproducible to summarize their learning. Assess the information to see if they have mastered the material, then differentiate your instruction as necessary.

Sequence

☑ **STEP 1:** Choose a topic for the classroom field trip.

☑ **STEP 2:** Research images, descriptions, and definitions about the topic and place them on large sheets of chart paper. For the topic of stages of human development, you might have the following stations: 1. The Life Cycle, 2. Before Birth, 3. Late Childhood, 4. Adolescence, 5. Young Adulthood, and 6. Late Adulthood.

MATERIALS

images and text to support a topic, chart paper and marker, a copy of Classroom Field Trip Guide reproducible (page 23) for each student, pens or pencils, sticky notes, timer, notebook paper (optional)

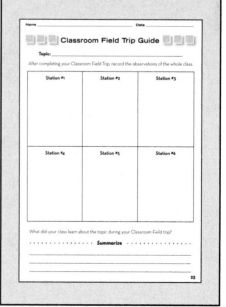

STEP 3: Number each sheet of chart paper and place a sheet at a different station around the classroom. Be sure to allow space for groups to move through and around the stations.

STEP 4: Distribute a copy of the Classroom Field Trip Guide reproducible to each student.

STEP 5: Separate students into as many groups as there are stations. Give each group sticky notes to place on the chart paper display at each station.

STEP 6: To begin, assign each group to a different station and set a timer for 3–4 minutes. More in-depth topics may need more time. Each group studies the information and completes the Classroom Field Trip Guide reproducible for the station. Before leaving, they record their comments on sticky notes and attach the notes to the chart paper.

STEP 7: When the timer goes off, each group rotates to the next station.

STEP 8: Repeat the process until each group has visited all the stations.

STEP 9: Have groups write a summary statement on the Classroom Field Trip Guide reproducible and share it with the whole class.

STEP 10: Ask each group to record the observations of the other groups on the back of the reproducible.

Classroom Field Trip Guide

Topic: _____

Station #1	Station #2	Station #3
Station #4	Station #5	Station #6

What did your class learn about the topic during your classroom field trip?

> > > > > > > > > > > > > > > > > *Summarize* < < < < < < < < < < < < < < < < < <

_____

_____

_____

Record the observations of the whole class on the back of this sheet.

CLOZE

Purpose

The cloze strategy increases students' comprehension and understanding of content.

Why It Works

The cloze strategy is effective because students have multiple opportunities to learn new material. They work individually, then with a partner, then as a whole class to determine the best possible answer and learn new material. Cloze promotes discussion and consensus building and can be based on your class's reading level.

ASSESSMENT OPTION

Formative Assessment

After teaching a topic, you can use the cloze strategy in the middle of a unit to gauge your students' understanding of the content. If students are able to complete the blanks with 80 percent accuracy, you know they can move to the next topic.

MATERIALS

text related to a topic (maximum of 300 words)

Sequence

STEP 1: Prior to teaching a unit, or while teaching it, decide on a suitable topic to use to check your students' understanding of it.

STEP 2: Select a text related to the topic that's on an appropriate level for your class. Any text can be used for a cloze activity, but try to limit the passage to 300 words.

STEP 3: Retype the text or copy and paste it into a document on the computer.

STEP 4: Leave the first and last sentences of the text intact.

STEP 5: Choose key words to delete from the text. Make sure to choose words that are fundamental to comprehending the topic. The number of words you delete is not important; what really matters is the words you choose.

STEP 6: Replace the deleted words with blank lines of equal length. Then you have the following two options:

    a. Have students write the missing word in the blank (see Example 1).

    b. Provide two possible answers for students to choose from (see Example 2).

STEP 7: Create a double-sided copy of the cloze activity for each student and distribute it.

STEP 8: Read the text to students, then have them independently complete the cloze on the first side of the sheet.

STEP 9: Ask students to share their work with a partner, discussing their answers and coming to a consensus on the best possible word choice.

STEP 10: Lead a discussion in which you provide the correct words so students can check their work.

STEP 11: Have students turn the reproducible over and fill in the same cloze text on the back to demonstrate mastery of the learning.

Example 1: Cloze on earthquakes

Most people living in California have at one time or another experienced an earthquake. Without warning, they wake up in the middle of the night because of the sometimes violent, sometimes slow rolling motion of the _____ ; at other times, they may be driving on the freeway, walking in the mall, or even just watching television when an earthquake occurs. So what causes them? Why do earthquakes feel so different from one another? Earthquakes are the earth's natural means of releasing _____. When the earth's _____ move against each other, stress is put on the _____. When this stress is great enough, the lithosphere breaks or _____. Imagine holding a pencil horizontally. If you were to apply a force to both ends of the pencil by pushing down on them, you would see the pencil bend. After enough force was applied, the pencil would break in the middle, releasing the _____ you have put on it. The earth's _____ acts in the same way. As the _____ move, they put forces on themselves and each other. When the force is large enough, the crust is forced to _____. When the break occurs, the stress is released as energy, which moves through the earth in the form of waves, which we feel and call an earthquake.

Example 2: Cloze on earthquakes with possible answers

Most people living in California have at one time or another experienced an earthquake. Without warning, they wake up in the middle of the night because of the sometimes violent, sometimes slow rolling motion of the _____ (ocean, earth) ; at other times, they may be driving on the freeway, walking in the mall, or even just watching television when an earthquake occurs. So what causes them? Why do earthquakes feel so different from one another? Earthquakes are the earth's natural means of releasing _____ (oxygen, stress). When the earth's _____ (currents, plates) move against each other, stress is put on the _____ (atmosphere, lithosphere). When this stress is great enough, the lithosphere breaks or _____ (shifts, solidifies). Imagine holding a pencil horizontally. If you were to apply a force to both ends of the pencil by pushing down on them, you would see the pencil bend. After enough force was applied, the pencil would break in the middle, releasing the _____ (stress, plates) you have put on it. The earth's _____ (ocean, crust) acts in the same way. As the _____ (plates, currents) move, they put forces on themselves and each other. When the force is large enough, the crust is forced to _____ (break, harden). When the break occurs, the stress is released as energy, which moves through the earth in the form of waves, which we feel and call an earthquake.

Check-in Assessments for Differentiated Lessons © 2012 by Troy Strayer & Beverly Strayer • Scholastic Teaching Resources

CONSENSUS LEARNING

Purpose

The Consensus Learning strategy allows students to prioritize and exercise choice in their learning.

Why It Works

At the beginning of a unit where there are multiple cause/effect/event factors, allowing students to choose a topic they want to learn more about increases their interest in the lesson and their ownership of the learning.

ASSESSMENT OPTIONS

Formative Assessment

During the unit, you can monitor students' understanding of the areas they suggested for further study. Because their interest has been aroused, students' answers will show depth and an understanding of the learning.

Summative Assessment

When the unit is concluded, you can provide students with the original list of causes and have them re-prioritize it and provide their justification for the new ranking.

MATERIALS

paper, pen or marker, scissors, an envelope, and Consensus Learning Ranking Sheet reproducible (page 31) for each group, material on selected topic

Sequence

✔ **STEP 1:** Choose a topic that is conducive to cause/effect learning; for example, the causes and effects of global warming.

✔ **STEP 2:** Create a sheet that lists the causes and briefly describes each one (see the example on pages 29–30). Cut the causes and descriptions into strips. Place a set of strips in an envelope.

✔ **STEP 3:** Separate students into groups and give each group an envelope and a Consensus Learning Ranking Sheet reproducible. Have each group read, discuss, and rank the causes according to its interest, and record the decisions on the reproducible.

✔ **STEP 4:** Hold a class discussion using the information from the completed reproducibles to identify the top three choices. Make sure the entire class reaches a consensus; this will be the focus of the unit.

✔ **STEP 5:** Gather materials on the selected topics and decide on instruction methods; for example, direct instruction, collaborative learning, or individual learning.

Example: Causes of the Civil War

Sectionalism

The growing gap between slave and free states was indicative of the changes occurring in each region. While the South was devoted to a plantation economy with a slow growth in industry, the North was characterized by industrialization, the development of large urban areas, and an ever-growing population of immigrants from diverse countries. This rise in population ensured Northern dominance in Congress and the potential of the election of a Northern, potentially anti-slavery, president.

The Abolitionist Movement

The issue of slavery was brought to prominence by the rise of the abolitionist movement in the 1820s and 1830s. In the North, abolitionists believed that slavery was morally wrong rather than just a social evil. Abolitionists varied in their beliefs: Some thought that all slaves should be freed immediately (William Lloyd Garrison, Frederick Douglas); some called for gradual emancipation (Theodore Weld, Arthur Tappan), and some simply wanted to stop the spread of slavery and its influence (Abraham Lincoln).

Abolitionists fought for the end of the "peculiar institution" and supported anti-slavery stands such as the Free State movement in Kansas. Abolitionists and Southerners battled over the morality of slavery, with both sides frequently citing biblical sources. In 1852, the abolitionist cause received increased attention following the publication of the anti-slavery novel *Uncle Tom's Cabin*. Written by Harriet Beecher Stowe, the book aided in turning the public against the Fugitive Slave Act of 1850. President Abraham Lincoln reportedly referred to Harriet Beecher Stowe as "the little woman who wrote the book that made this great war."

The Expansion of Slavery

Another political issue that helped move the nation towards conflict was the debate over slavery in the western territories won during the Mexican-American War. Congress had dealt with this issue earlier, in 1820, when it passed the Missouri Compromise, which allowed slavery in the Louisiana Purchase territory south of 36°30'N latitude. Then, in 1856, Representative David Wilmot attempted to prevent slavery in the new territories when he introduced the Wilmot Proviso in Congress. After extensive debate, it was defeated.

In 1850, the question of the expansion of slavery arose again. The Compromise of 1850 said that the issue of slavery in the unorganized lands (largely present-day Arizona and New Mexico) won from Mexico could be decided by popular sovereignty. This meant that the local people and their territorial legislatures would decide by vote whether slavery would be permitted. Many thought that this decision had solved the issue until it was raised again in 1854 with the passage of the Kansas-Nebraska Act.

Causes of the Civil War (continued)

States' Rights

The Southern states turned to the argument of states' rights to protect slavery. They threatened to nullify federal laws in an attempt to keep their way of life intact without federal interference. They also argued that the federal government was prohibited by the Tenth Amendment from prohibiting slaveholders from taking their "property" into a new territory. The Southern states also said that the federal government was not allowed to interfere with slavery in those states where it already existed.

Tariffs

The difference in the economies and lifestyles of the North and South was apparent in the debate over tariffs. There was dissension between the Northern and the Southern states over the matter of protective tariffs, or import duties on manufactured goods. The vast majority of American industry was located in the North, and Northern industries wanted high tariffs to protect their factories and laborers from cheaper European products. The economy of the plantation-based Southern states was based on exports, such as cotton, and the importation of manufactured goods. Because of tariffs, Southerners had to pay higher prices for goods in order to subsidize Northern manufacturing profits.

The money collected from these tariffs was used to fund public projects in the North, such as improvements to roads, bridges and canals. From 1789 to 1845, the North received five times the amount of money that was spent on projects in Southern states.

The tension caused by the passage of various tariff bills eventually led South Carolina to declare the tariff laws null and void. John C. Calhoun, a Senator from South Carolina and Vice-President under Andrew Jackson, proposed secession from the Union because of "unfair" federal tariffs.

Election of Abraham Lincoln

The presidential election of 1860 proved to be pivotal in dividing the Northern and Southern states. The votes of Southern Democrats were split between Stephen Douglas who represented Northern Democrats, John C. Breckinridge who represented Southern Democrats, and John C. Bell who represented former Whigs in the border states. The lack of a candidate with national appeal signaled that change was coming. Representing the newly formed Republican Party, an anti-slavery party, was Abraham Lincoln.

Sectionalism again prevailed as Lincoln won the North, Breckinridge won the South, and Bell won the border states. Douglas claimed Missouri and part of New Jersey. Because of the growing northern population, the Republican Party, and thus the North as a whole, had accomplished what the South had always feared. Representatives from Northern or free states now had complete control of the government

Check-in Assessments for Differentiated Lessons © 2012 by Troy Strayer & Beverly Strayer • Scholastic Teaching Resources

Name _____   Date _____

Consensus Learning Ranking Sheet

Group Members: _____ , _____ ,

_____ , _____

Topic: _____

Cause #1: _____ Reason(s)
Cause #2: _____ Reason(s)
Cause #3: _____ Reason(s)
Cause #4: _____ Reason(s)

DRAW WHAT'S ON MY MIND

Purpose

The Draw What's on My Mind strategy allows students to combine prior knowledge with new learning in order to comprehend new content.

Why It Works

In this strategy, students use pictures and words to express their prior knowledge about a topic, allowing them to apply their experiences to their learning. They then work collaboratively, sharing and explaining their drawings, which increases their comprehension and retention of the material.

ASSESSMENT OPTION

Summative Assessment

After daily instruction or at the end of a unit, you can have students draw a final picture showing the major details. You can leave the Details column on the reproducible blank and make students responsible for completing it, or you can provide the details and have them add a description based on their knowledge of the topic.

Sequence

✔ **STEP 1:** Before beginning a lesson on new content, distribute a copy of the Draw What's on My Mind reproducible to each student.

✔ **STEP 2:** Have students draw what they know about a term or topic related to the new content in the top box on the reproducible. Make sure that they have enough prior knowledge of the term or topic so they can draw a representation of it.

MATERIALS

Draw What's on My Mind reproducible (page 34), colored pencils, sheet of notebook paper (optional)

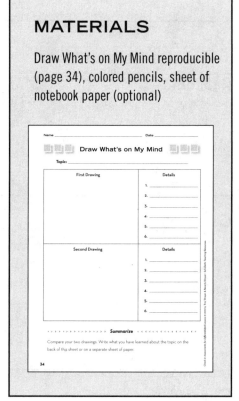

Check-in Assessments for Differentiated Lessons © 2012 by Troy Strayer & Beverly Strayer • Scholastic Teaching Resources

☑ **STEP 3:** Tell students to explain in the corresponding Details column of the reproducible why they drew what they did.

☑ **STEP 4:** Ask partners to explain their drawings to each other.

☑ **STEP 5:** Use the drawings to help determine the instructional strategies you want to use to teach students about the topic.

☑ **STEP 6:** During the instruction portion of your lesson, have students draw a second picture, adding details they have learned.

☑ **STEP 7:** Have students explain their second drawing to the same partner, pointing out their additions or deletions.

☑ **STEP 8:** Finally, on the back of the reproducible or on a separate sheet of paper, have students write a summary that compares their drawings and demonstrates their understanding.

Name _____   Date _____

Draw What's on My Mind

Topic: _____

First Drawing	Details
	1. _____
	2. _____
	3. _____
	4. _____
	5. _____
	6. _____
Second Drawing	**Details**
	1. _____
	2. _____
	3. _____
	4. _____
	5. _____
	6. _____

➤ ➤ ➤ ➤ ➤ ➤ ➤ ➤ ➤ ➤ ➤ ➤ ➤ ➤ *Summarize* ◄ ◄ ◄ ◄ ◄ ◄ ◄ ◄ ◄ ◄ ◄ ◄ ◄ ◄ ◄ ◄

Compare your two drawings. Write what you have learned about the topic on the

back of this sheet or on a separate sheet of paper.

Check-in Assessments for Differentiated Lessons © 2012 by Troy Strayer & Beverly Strayer • Scholastic Teaching Resources

ENTRY PASS

Purpose

Entry Pass is a way to introduce your students to new material by engaging them when they enter the classroom.

Why It Works

This strategy is a way to differentiate content and process by introducing them before you teach the lesson. Students formulate answers based on their prior knowledge and discuss their thoughts with fellow students and the teacher. Later, students revisit their answers and correct any misconceptions, which leads to a deeper understanding of the content.

ASSESSMENT OPTIONS

Formative Assessment

As students learn the material to answer a question on the Entry Pass, you can ask them to explain their answer either individually—on a whiteboard, for example—or with a partner.

Summative Assessment

At the end of the period, this strategy transitions well into an Exit Pass. Have students individually answer the questions a second time (on the back of their original sheet) and place the sheet in an Exit Pass container for you to review.

MATERIALS

sheet of Entry Pass questions, container(s)

Sequence

✔ **STEP 1:** Create a summative assessment for the unit.

✔ **STEP 2:** Organize the questions in the order in which you will teach them in your lessons.

✓ **STEP 3:** Create the Entry Pass questions. Print the questions for each lesson on a separate sheet of paper and make a copy for each student. The example on pages 37–38 shows an Algebra I summative assessment divided into daily lessons.

✓ **STEP 4:** Place Entry Passes in a container beside your door.

✓ **STEP 5:** Have students take an Entry Pass as they enter the room.

✓ **STEP 6:** Ask students to work individually or in pairs to answer the questions on the Entry Pass as soon as they sit down. The time you allow for the task depends on the complexity of the questions.

✓ **STEP 7:** As you teach the lesson, tell students to correct any answers and/or add to their existing answers.

OPTIONAL: EXIT PASS

✓ **STEP 8:** After the lesson, you can have students answer the questions a second time on the back of their Entry Pass. For this reason, when you create the Entry Passes, write the same set of questions on each side of the sheet.

✓ **STEP 9:** Collect the two sets of questions and answers from students as they exit the classroom.

Example: Algebra I Summative Assessment divided into daily lessons

ALGEBRA I Chapter 5 Test

Name:_____ Date: _____ Period: _____

(Lesson 1)

1. Put the following equation into slope-intercept form and graph the line.

   $3y - 15 = 2x$

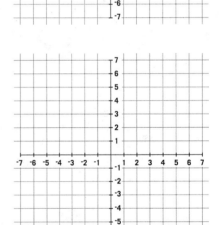

   Write an equation of the line that passes through the point and has the given slope.

   Write the equation in slope-intercept form. Circle your answers!!

2. $m = 3$, y–int $= -7$

3. $(0, -5)$ $m = \frac{1}{3}$

4. $(-2, 6)$, $m = 4$

5. Solve each equation for y, then graph the equation.

   a. $2x + y = 3$

   Equation: _____

   b. $4y = 2x - 8$

   Equation: _____

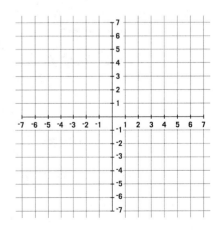

(Lesson 2)

6. Find the x– intercept of each equation.

   (Coordinate)

   a. $5x - 2y = 10$ _____

   b. $2x - 3y = 9$ _____

7. Find the x– and y– intercept of the equation and graph the line using the intercepts.

   $3x + 8y = 24$ x– intercept _____

                           y– intercept _____

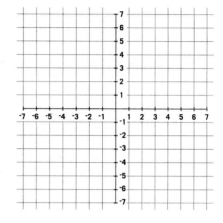

(Lesson 3)

8. Rewrite each equation into slope–intercept form. State the m (slope) and b (y– intercept).

   a. $3x + 5y = 15$ Equation: _____ $m =$ _____
                                                       $b =$ _____

   b. $y - 2x = 5$ Equation: _____ $m =$ _____
                                                       $b =$ _____

   c. $2x - 3y + 6 = 0$ Equation: _____ $m =$ _____
                                                       $b =$ _____

Write the slope-intercept form of the equation of the line that passes through two points. Circle your answers!!

   9. (2, 3), (6, 11)   **10.** (1, –7), (3, –15)

(Lesson 4)

Write the point-slope form of the equation of the line that passes through two points. Circle your answers!!

   11. (1, 2), (2, 4)   **12.** (–5, 6), (–6, 1)

Put the following equations into standard form. Circle your answers!!

   13. $3y - 12 = 4x$ **14.** $4x - 24 = 2y$ **15.** $y - 5x = 12$

   16. What is the slope of the line that is parallel to $3y + 4x = 12$?   _____

   What is the slope of the line that is perpendicular to $3y + 4x = 12$?   _____

Check-in Assessments for Differentiated Lessons © 2012 by Troy Strayer & Beverly Strayer • Scholastic Teaching Resources

GALLERY WALK

Purpose

A Gallery Walk introduces students to important vocabulary or topics they will learn throughout a new unit. It also provides students with pertinent information that will assist them in making meaning of the content during the learning.

Why It Works

This strategy encourages student discussion and movement to activate prior knowledge. It also allows students to preview important vocabulary and topics covered during the course of the unit.

ASSESSMENT OPTIONS

Pre-Assessment

By circulating around the room and listening to the discussions, you will be able to determine which words or topics need more in-depth instruction during the unit. You can adapt subsequent lessons based on what students already know about the topic.

Formative Assessment

Keep the Gallery Walk on display and refer to it as you teach. During the unit, you can use it to check where students are in their understanding of the information. You can accomplish this through assessment options such as a quick-write, a 25-word abstract, or a traditional quiz.

MATERIALS

index cards, marker, Gallery Walk reproducible (page 43), resources for topic, timer

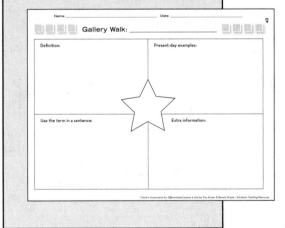

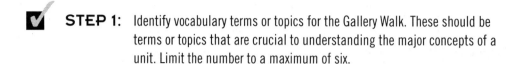

Sequence

✓ **STEP 1:** Identify vocabulary terms or topics for the Gallery Walk. These should be terms or topics that are crucial to understanding the major concepts of a unit. Limit the number to a maximum of six.

✓ **STEP 2:** Set up a workstation for each term or topic. Groups of students will be circulating from station to station, so create enough space between each station for everyone to move freely. See the sample setup below.

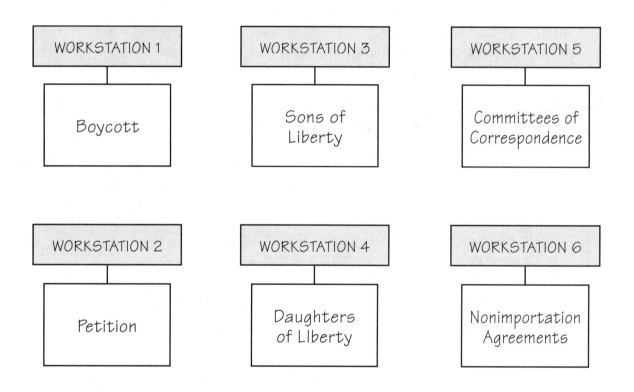

| WORKSTATION 1 | WORKSTATION 3 | WORKSTATION 5 |
| Boycott | Sons of Liberty | Committees of Correspondence |

| WORKSTATION 2 | WORKSTATION 4 | WORKSTATION 6 |
| Petition | Daughters of Liberty | Nonimportation Agreements |

✓ **STEP 3:** Customize a Gallery Walk reproducible for each term or topic and duplicate one for each student (see examples on page 42). Note the examples for Sons of Liberty and Daughters of Liberty; the reproducible was customized for these topics.

Check-in Assessments for Differentiated Lessons © 2012 by Troy Strayer & Beverly Strayer • Scholastic Teaching Resources

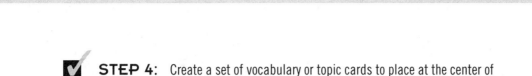

STEP 4: Create a set of vocabulary or topic cards to place at the center of each workstation.

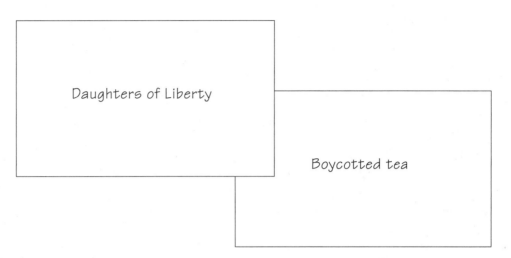

Daughters of Liberty

Boycotted tea

STEP 5: Provide students with short descriptions of the term or topic to assist them in completing the reproducible. Use textbooks, pictures, or brief print or Internet articles about the topic. Make enough copies for all students.

STEP 6: Separate students into groups of four or five, based on class size and the number of terms or topics.

STEP 7: Assign each group to a different workstation to start the Gallery Walk. Number the stations so students know where to go when they complete their first station. Explain that they will have 6–7 minutes to complete a reproducible for each term or topic at a workstation. When the time has elapsed, groups rotate to the next workstation.

STEP 8: Use a timer or an online stopwatch to time students at each workstation.

STEP 9: After each group has visited every workstation and completed the corresponding Gallery Walk reproducible, ask students to return to the original station to review and discuss the information their group has gathered.

Example

Gallery Walk: Colonial Protests to English Taxation

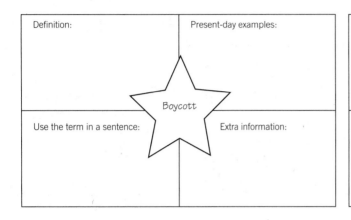

Definition:

Present-day examples:

Boycott

Use the term in a sentence:

Extra information:

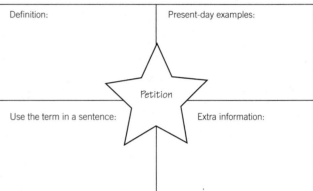

Definition:

Present-day examples:

Petition

Use the term in a sentence:

Extra information:

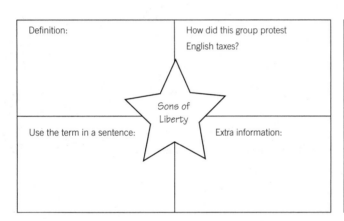

Definition:

How did this group protest English taxes?

Sons of Liberty

Use the term in a sentence:

Extra information:

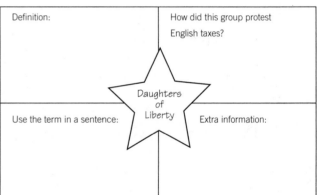

Definition:

How did this group protest English taxes?

Daughters of Liberty

Use the term in a sentence:

Extra information:

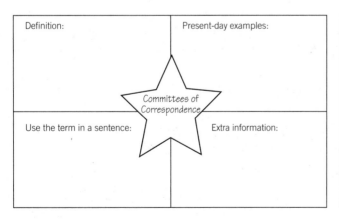

Definition:

Present-day examples:

Committees of Correspondence

Use the term in a sentence:

Extra information:

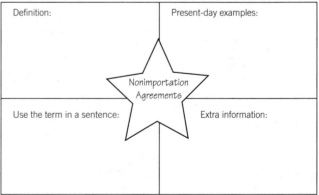

Definition:

Present-day examples:

Nonimportation Agreements

Use the term in a sentence:

Extra information:

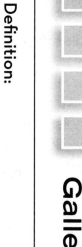

Gallery Walk: _____

Definition:

Present-day examples:

Use the term in a sentence:

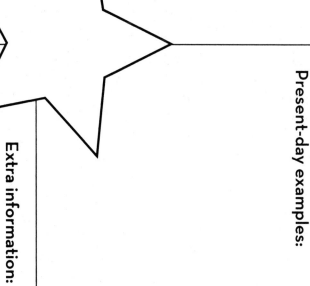

Extra information:

MAKE SENSE OF IT

Purpose

The Make Sense of It strategy builds vocabulary by actively engaging students in making meaningful sentences, while providing you with a means of assessing their knowledge of a topic.

Why It Works

Make Sense of It provides an opportunity for students to define and use upcoming vocabulary in their own words and then explain their work. This promotes higher-level thinking and strengthens comprehension, while also helping you assess your students' level of prior knowledge.

ASSESSMENT OPTIONS

Formative Assessment

After you have taught 3–5 vocabulary words, you can have students use the Make Sense of It reproducible to write a sentence using these words and explain their arrangement in the sentence. Students then share their sentences with a partner and ascertain whether they have used the vocabulary words correctly. If not, the writers make the necessary corrections.

Summative Assessment

At the completion of a unit, you can ask students to write detailed sentences demonstrating their knowledge of the vocabulary words.

MATERIALS

Make Sense of It reproducible (page 46)

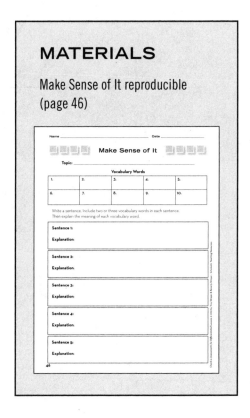

Sequence

☑ **STEP 1:** Compile a list of up to ten vocabulary words related to a lesson. The words should relate to both familiar and unfamiliar concepts.

☑ **STEP 2:** Have students create up to five sentences using the vocabulary words. Each sentence must contain at least two vocabulary words and no more than three.

☑ **STEP 3:** Ask students to explain what they believe the vocabulary words mean below each sentence. This will help their comprehension and allow you to determine their level of prior knowledge.

☑ **STEP 4:** After teaching the lesson, have students assess their sentences by writing **C** (for correct), **I** (for incorrect), or **N** (not certain) beside each one.

☑ **STEP 5:** Tell students to revise each incorrect sentence to make it correct. If students are uncertain about a sentence, direct them to consult with other students to verify its accuracy.

Student Sample: words related to a lesson on the Constitution

Name _____   Date _____

Make Sense of It

Topic: _____

Vocabulary Words

1.	2.	3.	4.	5.
6.	7.	8.	9.	10.

Write a sentence. Include two or three vocabulary words in each sentence.
Then explain the meaning of each vocabulary word.

Sentence 1:

Explanation:

Sentence 2:

Explanation:

Sentence 3:

Explanation:

Sentence 4:

Explanation:

Sentence 5:

Explanation:

Check-in Assessments for Differentiated Lessons © 2012 by Troy Strayer & Beverly Strayer • Scholastic Teaching Resources

NARROW IT DOWN

Purpose

The Narrow It Down strategy promotes individual thinking and discussion to help students learn about a new topic through print, an image, or a video.

Why It Works

This strategy allows students to put new learning into their own words and discuss their interpretation of the material. This increases their interest in the lesson and ensures that you address their readiness prior to designing lessons to teach the material.

ASSESSMENT OPTIONS

Formative Assessment

During the lesson, you can ask students to complete the steps of Narrow It Down to gather data about their learning. Circulate around the room to monitor students' thinking processes to see if they understand the content and can move to the next task in the lesson.

Summative Assessment

At the end of the lesson, you can ask students to summarize their learning by completing the steps in Narrow It Down. Collect students' responses and use them to guide your instruction for the following day.

MATERIALS

written description, video clip, or image of topic; Narrow It Down reproducible (page 49), printed material about topic (optional)

Sequence

☑ **STEP 1:** Choose a topic.

☑ **STEP 2:** Select a brief written description, a video clip, or an image of the topic to present to the class. Customize the Narrow It Down reproducible by completing the first line as follows:

- After reading the description of (topic)
- After viewing the clip about (topic)
- After seeing the picture of (topic)

☑ **STEP 3:** Present the information on the topic to students. If you're using print material, you can give a copy of the description to each student.

☑ **STEP 4:** Distribute a copy of the Narrow It Down reproducible to each student and have them write six words describing what they read or saw.

☑ **STEP 5:** Separate students into small groups to share and discuss the words they chose.

☑ **STEP 6:** Tell groups to narrow the words to the three best descriptions.

☑ **STEP 7:** Allow time for each group to share its best descriptions with the whole class.

☑ **STEP 8:** Have the other groups add any new words to their list.

☑ **STEP 9:** Tell each student to make a new list by choosing the three best words from the class discussion.

☑ **STEP 10:** Finally, ask students to explain why these words best summarize the topic.

Student Sample: Narrow It Down for a video clip on weathering

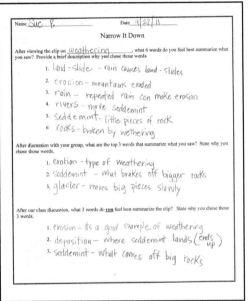

Check-in Assessments for Differentiated Lessons © 2012 by Troy Strayer & Beverly Strayer • Scholastic Teaching Resources

 # Narrow It Down

Which six words do you feel best summarize what you read or saw in _____
_____? Write a brief description about why you chose those words.
    (book or video title)

Word	Explanation
1.	
2.	
3.	
4.	
5.	
6.	

Discuss the words with your group. Combine your words and then choose the
three words that best summarize the information you read or saw.

1.	2.	3.

Discuss these words with the class. Then choose the three words that you feel best
summarize the information you read or saw. Explain your reasons for choosing these words.

Word	Explanation
1.	
2.	
3.	

Check-in Assessments for Differentiated Lessons © 2012 by Troy Strayer & Beverly Strayer • Scholastic Teaching Resources

SHARING IDEAS

Purpose

The Sharing Ideas strategy encourages students to collaborate to gain knowledge and perspective on a topic.

Why It Works

Often students enter our classrooms without prior knowledge of the material that will be taught. Providing them with a visual image or a written passage on a topic allows you to determine students' readiness level before teaching a lesson. Working collaboratively also increases students' retention of the material.

ASSESSMENT OPTION

Formative Assessment

You can use the Sharing Ideas strategy during the lesson to analyze a student's original responses. After students record their original responses, teach the material and have them add information or make corrections to their responses. Then ask students to share their additions and corrections with a partner or a small group. Circulate around the room, monitoring their discussions.

MATERIALS

visual or written material about a topic, Sharing Ideas reproducible (page 52), highlighters

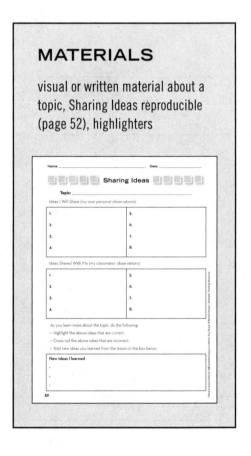

Check-in Assessments for Differentiated Lessons © 2012 by Troy Strayer & Beverly Strayer • Scholastic Teaching Resources

Sequence

✓ **STEP 1:** Research the topic to find a visual image or a passage for students to preview. Make a copy for each student and distribute it along with the Sharing Ideas reproducible.

✓ **STEP 2:** After students view the visual or read the passage, tell them to record up to four observations on the Sharing Ideas reproducible. Note that the reproducible allows you to increase or decrease that number.

✓ **STEP 3:** Have students move around the room, sharing their ideas and adding their classmates' ideas to their reproducible in the Ideas Shared With Me section.

✓ **STEP 4:** Ask students to raise their hand when they are finished.

✓ **STEP 5:** Ask students to repeat steps 3 and 4 with different classmates until the Ideas Shared With Me section of their reproducible is complete.

✓ **STEP 6:** When students return to their seats, instruct them to add important information and make corrections to their original responses during the lesson.

Student Sample: Sharing Ideas on the topic of Japan

Name _____   Date _____

 # Sharing Ideas

Topic: _____

Ideas I Will Share (my own personal observations):

1.	5.
2.	6.
3.	7.
4.	8.

Ideas Shared With Me (my classmates' observations)

1.	5.
2.	6.
3.	7.
4.	8.

As you learn more about the topic, do the following:

• Highlight the above ideas that are correct.

• Cross out the above ideas that are incorrect.

• Add new ideas you learned from the lesson in the box below.

New ideas I learned

•

•

•

Check-in Assessments for Differentiated Lessons © 2012 by Troy Strayer & Beverly Strayer • Scholastic Teaching Resources

WHAT DO YOU KNOW ABOUT . . . ?

Purpose

The What Do You Know About . . . ? strategy develops students' knowledge of a concept through conversation and movement.

Why It Works

This strategy focuses on students' readiness and learning styles and fosters collaboration. Also, by suggesting future topics for instruction, you pique students' interest. They decide what they will learn in addition to what you would normally teach.

ASSESSMENT OPTION

Formative Assessment

After completing a lesson objective or an essential question, you can have students complete a What Do You Know About . . .? reproducible. To gauge their mastery of the material, circulate around the room to listen to interviewees' responses and observe interviewers' recorded responses. If many students are providing incorrect information, it will be necessary to reteach the material.

MATERIALS

What Do You Know About . . . ? reproducible (page 55); What Do You Know About . . .? Summarizer reproducible (page 56); timer

Sequence

☑ **STEP 1:** Choose a topic.

☑ **STEP 2:** Pass out a What Do You Know About . . .? reproducible to each student.

☑ **STEP 3:** Tell students to interview three or four classmates about the topic and record what they find out on the reproducible. As the student sample below shows, you can also ask students to "interview" the characters from a story or a book.

☑ **STEP 4:** Remind students to write the name of each person in the first column of the reproducible and to record the information from each interview in the remaining columns.

☑ **STEP 5:** Set a time limit for each interview and use a timer to help students keep track of the time.

☑ **STEP 6:** Have students return to their seats and use the information from their interviews to complete the What Do You Know About . . . ? Summarizer. Use their responses to determine topics for future instruction.

Student Sample: interview of four characters from *Wicked Lovely*

What Do You Know About. . . Topic: Wicked Lovely			
Person	**Detail #1**	**Detail #2**	**Detail #3**
Aislinn	Can see fairies	Loves Seth	Becomes the Summer Queen
Keenan	Is king of the Summer Faeries	Needs Aislinn	Queen Beira is his mother
Seth	Loves Aislinn	Gets kidnapped by Queen Beira	Lives in a train
Donia	Loves Keenan	Picked the cold for Keenan	Becomes the Winter Queen

Check-in Assessments for Differentiated Lessons © 2012 by Troy Strayer & Beverly Strayer • Scholastic Teaching Resources

Name _____ Date _____

What Do You Know About . . . ?

Topic: _____

Person	Detail #1	Detail #2	Detail #3

What Do You Know About . . . ?
Summarizer

Summarize what your classmates knew about the topic.

What details would you like to know more about?

What questions arose when you did your interviews?

Check-in Assessments for Differentiated Lessons © 2012 by Troy Strayer & Beverly Strayer • Scholastic Teaching Resources

WINDOW PANE

Purpose

In the Window Pane strategy, students share prior knowledge about a topic and then form a consensus for a definition or a description of it.

Why It Works

This strategy allows students to collaborate and come to a consensus on the definition of critical vocabulary or the meaning of an unfamiliar topic. Students' interest is engaged and learning styles are addressed as they explore the content of upcoming lessons.

ASSESSMENT OPTIONS

Pre-Assessment

Listening to group discussions and collecting the Window Pane templates will allow you to determine the depth that you need to give to the vocabulary or topic. If most students have a firm grasp of it, you can choose to devote more time to other material.

Formative Assessment

Window Pane can be used as a formative assessment during instruction to gauge where students are with any term or topic. For example, if you used the Window Pane to introduce a topic, you can use the strategy again after teaching it to ensure that students have learned the content.

MATERIALS

paper and marker to create Window Pane template; different-colored markers or pens, black markers or pens for each group member

Sequence

☑ **STEP 1:** Identify the vocabulary terms or topics you want students to explore.

☑ **STEP 2:** Determine how many students will be in each group and then create the template for them to use (see Examples 1, 2, and 3).

☑ **STEP 3:** Form groups and direct each group member to select a writing utensil of a color other than black. Explain that black ink will be used for the last step.

☑ **STEP 4:** Hand out a Window Pane template to each group. Tell each member to write his or her name or initials in a section of the Window Pane.

☑ **STEP 5:** Reveal the term or topic. Have students write everything they know about it in their section of the Window Pane, using their individual color.

☑ **STEP 6:** Tell students to establish the talking order of the group members by taking numbers.

☑ **STEP 7:** Student #1 shares his or her information. The other students circle things they have written in common with Student #1. They repeat this process until everyone has shared.

☑ **STEP 8:** Using commonalities, the group works together to reach a consensus on a definition or description of the term or topic and writes it in the center of the Window Pane in black ink.

SUPPLEMENTAL OPTION:

When all groups have completed the Window Pane, use the Gallery Walk strategy on pages 39–43 to allow students to gain a different perspective about the term or topic.

Check-in Assessments for Differentiated Lessons © 2012 by Troy Strayer & Beverly Strayer • Scholastic Teaching Resources

EXAMPLE 1:
Window Pane for 3 Group Members

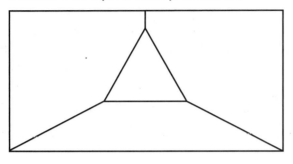

EXAMPLE 2:
Window Pane for 4 Group Members

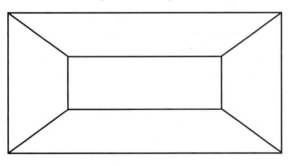

EXAMPLE 3:
Window Pane for 5 Group Members

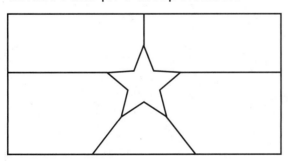

Student Sample: Window Pane on effective groups (3 students)

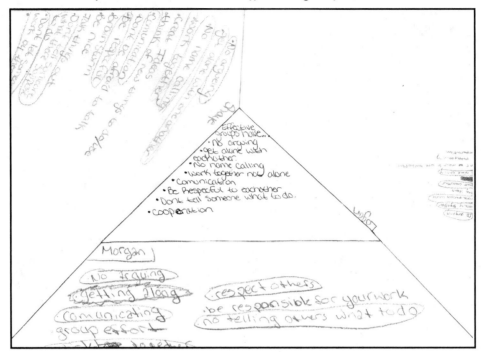

Student Sample: Window Pane on effective groups (4 students)

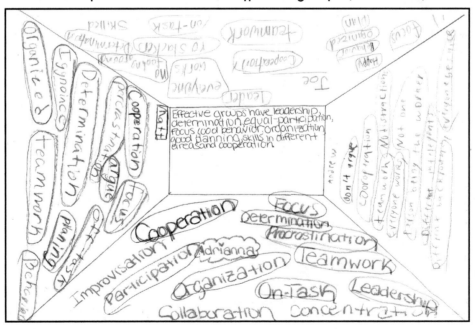

Quick Assessments to Wrap Up Lessons

Summarization is one of the most underused teaching techniques we have today, yet research has shown that it yields some of the greatest leaps in comprehension and long-term retention of information.

~ RICK WORMELI, *SUMMARIZATION IN ANY SUBJECT*

SUMMARY FRAME

Purpose

Using a Summary Frame increases students' comprehension by focusing their learning and understanding within a controlled framework.

Why It Works

A Summary Frame is an excellent strategy to familiarize your students with summarizing. It has three purposes: 1) to provide a framework to facilitate students' understanding and responses; 2) to give students a structured format to follow for writing a content-area activity; and 3) to scaffold students' ability to use independent summarization strategies.

The frame provides scaffolding for those who have difficulty weeding out unimportant information. Preparing your own Summary Frame presents a model for students and helps them summarize successfully.

ASSESSMENT OPTION

Formative Assessment

After a lesson, you can use the Summary Frame to check where students are in their understanding of the information. For a graded assignment, score the Summary Frames against the rubric on page 63. To differentiate by readiness, provide a Summary Frame with fewer blanks. As those students progress, you can increase the number of blanks.

MATERIALS

Summary Frame reproducible (page 64), rubric (page 63), pens or pencils

Check-in Assessments for Differentiated Lessons © 2012 by Troy Strayer & Beverly Strayer • Scholastic Teaching Resources

Rubric

EXPERT	PROGRESSING	NOVICE
Student completes all parts of the summary frame accurately.	Student completes most parts of the summary frame accurately.	Student completes few parts of the summary frame accurately.
Student has an excellent grasp of the learning.	Student has an adequate grasp of the learning.	Student has a minimal grasp of the learning.
Student uses only important information in the summary frame.	Student usually uses important information in the summary frame.	Student uses unimportant information in the summary frame.

Sequence

☑ **STEP 1:** Display a Summary Frame reproducible on the overhead or a document camera and model how to complete it.

☑ **STEP 2:** Give a copy of the reproducible to each student. Instruct them to complete the Summary Frame based on the day's learning (see the example below).

☑ **STEP 3:** Have students share their Summary Frame with a partner.

☑ **STEP 4:** If you are using the Summary Frame as a summative assessment, use the rubric to score students' work. Ask two pairs to form a square to share their Summary Frames. Then tell them to choose one Summary Frame to share with the entire class.

Example

Topic: Measurement in Math Class

Today, I learned about _area_ in _math_ class.

The first thing I learned was _that area is used to measure how much carpet or tile you might need in a room_.

Next, I learned _that area is the inside of a two-dimensional shape_.

After that, I learned _the formula for area: area = length x width_.

Tomorrow, I want to learn more about _area and how I can use that information when I get out of school_.

Name _____ Date _____

Summary Frame

Today, I learned about _____ in _____ class.

The first thing I learned was _____

_____ .

Next, I learned _____

_____ .

After that, I learned _____

_____ .

Tomorrow, I want to learn more about _____

_____ .

- -

Name _____ Date _____

Summary Frame

Today, I learned about _____ in _____ class.

The first thing I learned was _____

_____ .

Next, I learned _____

_____ .

After that, I learned _____

_____ .

Tomorrow, I want to learn more about _____

_____ .

3-2-1 BLAST OFF!

Purpose

This strategy engages students in analyzing, synthesizing, and reflecting upon their learning.

Why It Works

The 3-2-1 Blast Off! strategy emphasizes the importance of reflection in the learning process. This summarizer gives students a framework for analyzing what they learned and synthesizing this new learning with previously learned material. This activity deepens students' learning because it requires them to use analysis and synthesis, which, according to Benjamin Bloom's taxonomy of learning, corresponds to higher levels of thinking than basic comprehension.

ASSESSMENT OPTIONS

Formative Assessment

During a unit of study, you can use the 3-2-1 Blast Off! strategy to check students' understanding of the material. Analyzing the reproducible will show you what each student knows and which students may need additional practice or instruction before the summative assessment.

Summative Assessment

You can also use this reproducible as a summative assessment for a unit of study to gain a clear picture of where your students are in relation to Common Core State Standards. This is a simple alternative for students who do not do well in a testing situation.

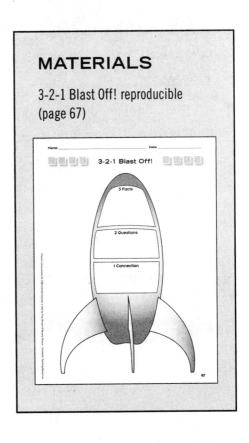

MATERIALS

3-2-1 Blast Off! reproducible (page 67)

Sequence

☑ **STEP 1:** Provide each student with a copy of the 3-2-1 Blast Off! reproducible.

☑ **STEP 2:** At the top of the rocket, have students write the three most important facts they learned about the topic.

☑ **STEP 3:** In the middle of the rocket, tell students to write two questions they still have about the topic. These questions should require more than a yes-or-no answer. If you are using this as a formative assessment, you may use the questions to plan instruction. If it is used as a summative assessment, you may meet with flexible, small groups to clear up questions or misconceptions.

☑ **STEP 4:** At the bottom of the rocket, ask students to write one way in which they can connect the new learning with material they have previously learned. (See the example below from a math lesson on prime numbers and factors.)

Example

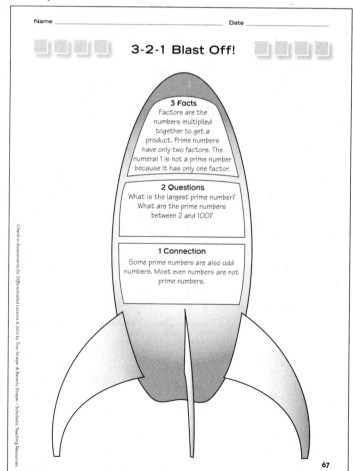

Student Samples: 3-2-1 Blast Off! on the topic of slavery

Check-in Assessments for Differentiated Lessons © 2012 by Troy Strayer & Beverly Strayer • Scholastic Teaching Resources

3-2-1 Blast Off!

3 Facts

2 Questions

1 Connection

ARTISTIC SUMMARY

Purpose

The Artistic Summary strategy is a summative assessment strategy that works well for students who lack confidence in their test-taking skills.

Why It Works

Summarizers usually involve writing, but Artistic Summary requires illustrating before any writing takes place. This is because most students show deeper comprehension when they are asked to summarize artistically. When students begin by creating a drawing, their written summaries improve greatly.

ASSESSMENT OPTIONS

Formative Assessment

At the end of a lesson, you can use the Artistic Summary strategy to assess students' understanding. Looking at students' illustrations and listening to their oral descriptions will tell you whether they are ready to proceed to the next lesson or concept. This summarizer is helpful when differentiating your lesson according to process. Not all learners are adept at putting their thoughts down on paper. It allows visual, tactile, and kinesthetic learners the opportunity to use their strengths to build a written or spoken answer.

Summative Assessment

You can use the Artistic Summary Rubric as the summative assessment at the end of a unit of study. It is an effective alternative to the traditional pencil-and-paper test.

MATERIALS

Artistic Summary Rubric (page 70); art materials, such as crayons, colored pencils, rulers, unlined sheets of paper, and so on

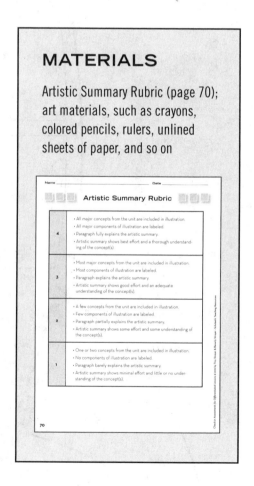

Check-in Assessments for Differentiated Lessons © 2012 by Troy Strayer & Beverly Strayer • Scholastic Teaching Resources

Sequence

☑ **STEP 1:** Decide whether to use Artistic Summary as a formative or summative assessment. This will determine the amount of time you allow for students to complete it. If you are using it as a formative assessment, it should take students about 15 minutes to do the illustration and another 15–20 minutes for the written or spoken part. If you are using it as a summative assessment, allow more time for students to do the illustration. You may also allow them to complete the illustration as homework. After checking it the next day, have students use it for the assessment. In this situation, it may take 15–30 minutes for the summative assessment.

☑ **STEP 2:** Set out the art materials.

☑ **STEP 3:** Inform students which topic they should summarize and tell them to create an illustration for their summary.

☑ **STEP 4:** When students are finished, provide time for all of them to explain their summaries to the rest of the class.

☑ **STEP 5:** Then, on a separate sheet of paper, have students write one paragraph explaining their artistic summary (see the example below).

Example

Topic: <u>Landforms</u>

In my artistic summary of landforms, I drew a mountain, a valley, a cliff, and a plateau. The valley, cliff, and plateau are formed by erosion. The mountain is formed by tectonic activity and deposition. Erosion, tectonic activity, and deposition take place over long periods of time.

☑ **STEP 6:** If you are using Artistic Summary as a summative assessment, score students' illustrations and paragraphs with the rubric.

Artistic Summary Rubric

4	• All major concepts from the unit are included in illustration. • All major components of illustration are labeled. • Paragraph fully explains the artistic summary. • Artistic summary shows best effort and a thorough understanding of the concept(s).
3	• Most major concepts from the unit are included in illustration. • Most components of illustration are labeled. • Paragraph explains the artistic summary. • Artistic summary shows good effort and an adequate understanding of the concept(s).
2	• A few concepts from the unit are included in illustration. • Few components of illustration are labeled. • Paragraph partially explains the artistic summary. • Artistic summary shows some effort and some understanding of the concept(s).
1	• One or two concepts from the unit are included in illustration. • No components of illustration are labeled. • Paragraph barely explains the artistic summary. • Artistic summary shows minimal effort and little or no understanding of the concept(s).

Check-in Assessments for Differentiated Lessons © 2012 by Troy Strayer & Beverly Strayer • Scholastic Teaching Resources

HIGH-FIVE SUMMARY

Purpose

The High-Five Summary strategy gives students an opportunity to summarize major concepts, focus on main ideas, and experience success.

Why it Works

The High-Five Summary works well because it requires little teacher preparation, and since there is little writing, it is more appealing to those students who struggle with writing.

ASSESSMENT OPTIONS

MATERIALS

paper and pencils or pens

Formative Assessment

As students are working, you can circulate and look for incorrect responses or misinformation. Work one-on-one with students to correct any errors or misconceptions.

You can also use the High-Five Summary to plan the next day's lesson. After reading the summaries, you know which students have mastered the concepts and which ones need additional time with the material. If the majority of the class has a misconception, you may reteach that concept the next day to the whole class. If there are only a few students who are having difficulty, you can meet with them either individually or in a small skill group.

Summative Assessment

Score the High-Five Summary on a 10-point scale. Assign 2 points for each complete, correct answer. Assign 1 point for each partial answer, and award 0 points for an incorrect response.

Sequence

✓ **STEP 1:** Identify the five key concepts of the lesson. Make sure you stress these key concepts throughout the lesson. (See the examples on page 73.)

✓ **STEP 2:** At the end of the lesson, have students trace their hand on a sheet of paper.

✓ **STEP 3:** Tell students to identify the five main points of the lesson and to write each main point inside one of the fingers on their tracing.

✓ **STEP 4:** Have students share their High-Five Summary with a partner.

✓ **STEP 5:** Collect the summaries and check them. If you are using the summaries as a formative assessment, plan the next day's lesson based on what the summaries reveal about students' understanding of the concepts. If you are using them as a summative assessment, you may assign a test grade or a project grade for students' understanding of the skill or concepts.

Student Samples:
High-Five Summary for a story

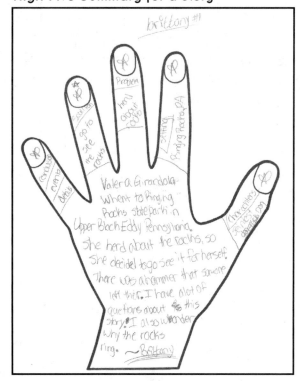

High-Five Summary for a lesson on cells

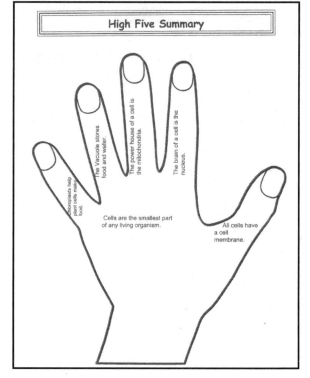

Check-in Assessments for Differentiated Lessons © 2012 by Troy Strayer & Beverly Strayer • Scholastic Teaching Resources

Examples

Topic: Cells

5 main points:

1. Everything is made of cells.
2. All cells have a nucleus.
3. Plant cells have a cell wall and chloroplasts.
4. Mitochondria are the powerhouses of the cell.
5. Vacuoles store food and water for the cell.

Topic: Geometry

Instruct students to draw five geometric figures and list one attribute of each. They may not draw a square, rectangle, triangle, or circle.

5 geometric figures

1. parallelogram: 2 pair of parallel sides
2. trapezoid: 1 pair of parallel sides
3. pentagon: sum of the angles equals 540 degrees
4. octagon: has eight sides (a stop sign)
5. heptagon: sum of the angles equals 900 degrees

Topic: Spanish Explorers

5 reasons for exploration:

1. to promote Christianity
2. to search for wealth
3. to gain new land
4. to find spices
5. to increase knowledge

Topic: Food Pyramid

5 main points:

1. Eat at least 6 ounces of whole-grain foods every day.
2. Eat 5 ounces of lean or low-fat meat or beans a day.
3. Eat 2½ cups of vegetables a day. Fresh is best.
4. Drink 3 cups of milk a day.
5. Eat 1½ cups of fruit a day. Fresh is best.

MONEY TALKS

Purpose

The Money Talks summarizer affords every student an opportunity to review essential content or concepts by stating the main points in paragraph form.

Why It Works

Some students write a book to answer an essay question when a few well-written, concise sentences would suffice. This summarizer forces students to eliminate nonessential information from their responses.

ASSESSMENT OPTIONS

MATERIALS

paper and pencils or pens

Formative Assessment

During the unit, you can use the Money Talks summarizer to check where students are in their understanding of the concepts or information you are teaching. Use that information to plan future instruction.

Summative Assessment

As a summative assessment, the Money Talks summarizer should also be used in place of essay questions. Its concise nature will save you time and drastically improve the quality of students' responses. When you use the Money Talks summarizer as a summative assessment, you may use the checklist below.

Money Talks Summarizer Checklist

Student is within $0.10 either way of the predetermined amount.	2 points
Student identifies most important concepts in the summary.	4 points
Student uses complete sentences in the summary.	2 points
Summary makes sense.	2 points

 Check-in Assessments for Differentiated Lessons © 2012 by Troy Strayer & Beverly Strayer • Scholastic Teaching Resources

Sequence

☑ STEP 1: Identify the number of words you want students to use to summarize the content or concept. Each word will be worth $0.10. *A, an,* and *the* do not count. Amounts between $1.50 and $3.50 are the most manageable (14–16 words/34–36 words). (See the examples below.)

☑ STEP 2: Create a prompt for the summary statement, for example: *Write a $2.40 summary of photosynthesis.* In this example, students must write a summary of photosynthesis using 23–25 words.

☑ STEP 3: Explain the rules to students and then give them the prompt.

☑ STEP 4: The first time you use this strategy, circulate to provide support while students are creating their summarizers.

☑ STEP 5: Have students reread their summary statement to be sure it makes sense and the word count is correct.

Examples

Cells ($3.00)

The cell of an animal has five major parts. The nucleus is the control center of the cell, the mitochondria is the powerhouse, the vacuole stores water and food, and the cytoplasm (which looks like jelly) holds the other parts of the cell together. **($3.10: within $0.10)**

Jamestown ($2.50)

Jamestown was the first permanent English settlement in America. The first group of settlers was made up of only 104 men and boys. The Powhatan Indians helped the colonists survive. **($2.50: within $0.10)**

NAME THAT WORD

Purpose

The Name That Word game actively involves every student in summarizing and reviewing essential content-area vocabulary.

Why It Works

This summarizer works well for several reasons, the first being that each student is actively involved in every question and every answer. It also shows students' understanding of content vocabulary because they must know the word to be able to give good clues during the summary.

ASSESSMENT OPTION

Formative Assessment

During the unit, you can use the Name That Word game to check where students are in their comprehension of important vocabulary. As you circulate during the game, you can take anecdotal notes to help you make instructional decisions for the next lesson or form small skill groups for remediation.

MATERIALS

paper and marker or pen, scissors

Sequence

☑ **STEP 1:** Identify the vocabulary terms or topics for the Name That Word game. These should be words that are crucial to understanding the major concepts of the unit. Limit the number of terms or topics to a maximum of 12.

☑ **STEP 2:** Create two lists, List A and List B, for students to use during the game (see examples on page 77).

☑ **STEP 3:** Model the game by playing it with a student (see Steps 4–7). (*Note:* Do not use the words on List A or List B.)

☑ **STEP 4:** Pair students and have them decide who will be Player A and who will be Player B.

✔ **STEP 5:** Give List A to Player A and List B to Player B. Give students a few minutes to look over their list to make sure they know the words. If a student does not know a word, give him or her time to check his or her notes or to meet with a peer who has the same list.

✔ **STEP 6:** At your signal, Player A gives clues to help Player B guess the first vocabulary word on List A. The actual word or any derivative of it may not be used as a clue.

✔ **STEP 7:** When Player B guesses the correct word, he or she gives clues to help Player A guess the first word on List B. This process continues until both players have correctly identified all the words on their respective lists.

✔ **STEP 8:** After the game is finished, check to see if students have questions.

Examples

Topic: Living Things

List A	List B
mitochondria	cells
nucleus	cell walls
vacuole	chloroplast
chlorophyll	ribosome
cell membrane	endoplasmic reticulum

Topic: Narrative

List A	List B
falling action	climax
setting	characters
rising action	foreshadowing
plot	tone
resolution	point of view

Topic: American Revolution

List A	List B
Tories	Green Mountain Boys
Boston Tea Party	Intolerable Acts
Valley Forge	Patriots
Loyalists	Fence Sitters
Articles of Confederation	Bunker Hill

Topic: Geometry

List A	List B
quadrilateral	isosceles triangle
obtuse angle	trapezoid
equilateral triangle	acute angle
rectangular prism	scalene triangle
sphere	right triangle

PASS-AROUND PARAGRAPH

Purpose

The Pass-Around Paragraph strategy helps students process information cooperatively and also reinforces collaborative writing in the content areas.

Why It Works

As students pass around the paragraph and read what each previous student has written, they gain a deeper understanding of the content. When they work together to write a concluding sentence, they analyze what was written and synthesize it.

ASSESSMENT OPTION

Formative Assessment

Even though the Pass-Around Paragraph is a cooperative strategy, you can build individual accountability into it. Have each student in a group use a different colored pencil. Looking at the individual sentences gives you a clear picture of each student's understanding of the content.

MATERIALS

different-colored pencils and a piece of paper for each group

Sequence

☑ **STEP 1:** After you have taught content or students have read a short passage, decide on a topic sentence that will help them summarize the material.

☑ **STEP 2:** Form groups of four or five students. Have each group number off from 1 to 4 for groups of four and from 1 to 5 for groups of five.

☑ **STEP 3:** Tell each group to write the topic sentence at the top of a sheet of paper. Student #1 writes the first detail sentence after the prompt or topic sentence. Student #2 reads Student #1's sentence and adds a second detail sentence, building on the first one, to the same sheet of paper. The contributing writer then reads aloud the entire paragraph. The process continues until each student in the group has contributed a sentence.

 Check-in Assessments for Differentiated Lessons © 2012 by Troy Strayer & Beverly Strayer • Scholastic Teaching Resources

STEP 4: After the last student has written a sentence, the entire paragraph is read aloud one more time. The group then works cooperatively to write a concluding sentence for the paragraph (see the examples below).

STEP 5: Have each group share its paragraph with the class.

Example 1

Group

Topic: Area and Perimeter

Area and perimeter are important concepts in math. Area is the space inside a two-dimensional shape. You can find area by multiplying a shape's length by its width. Perimeter is the distance around a shape. You find perimeter by adding the length of the sides together. You need to know the difference between area and perimeter if you are buying carpet or building a fence.

Students 1, 2, 3, and 4

Group

Example 2

Group

Topic: Similes and Metaphors

Authors use similes and metaphors to make their writing better. A simile uses <u>like</u> or <u>as</u> to compare. "He is as wise as an owl" is a simile. Metaphor is making a comparison without using <u>like</u> or <u>as</u>. "He is a machine" is an example of a metaphor. When you write, you should try to use similes or metaphors.

Students 1, 2, 3, and 4

Group

PASS-THE-BALL SUMMARY

Purpose

The Pass-the-Ball Summary provides an opportunity for each student to react to or summarize content while keeping track of what others say.

Why It Works

Many kinesthetic learners have few opportunities for movement in the traditional classroom. The Pass-the-Ball Summary, used successfully from kindergarten through 12th grade, gives the kinesthetic learner a chance to move and excel.

ASSESSMENT OPTION

Formative Assessment

After teaching a lesson, you can use the Pass-the-Ball Summary game to gain a general sense of students' understanding and comprehension of the material. As students are completing the summary, take anecdotal notes to help determine which students are ready to move on and which may need further instruction.

MATERIALS

inflatable beach ball
Note: With this activity, you should stress the importance of throwing the ball with care and of calling the person's name before tossing it.

Sequence

 STEP 1: Identify the topic(s) for the Pass-the-Ball Summary.

 STEP 2: Share the following rules of the game:

- Before carefully tossing the ball, a player names the person to whom he or she will toss it.

- After catching the ball, a player has 5 seconds to state an idea, fact, or concept about the topic from the lesson.

- Each student is permitted one pass (an opportunity not to answer). If the student cannot contribute on his or her next turn, the student must sit down.

Check-in Assessments for Differentiated Lessons © 2012 by Troy Strayer & Beverly Strayer • Scholastic Teaching Resources

- Once a student has had a turn to speak, he or she should not have another turn until everyone has spoken once.

- Players may not leave their place in the circle during the activity.

- Facts may not be repeated, so players must listen carefully.

STEP 3: Begin the game by restating the topic, then saying a student's name and tossing the ball to that student.

STEP 4: That student has 5 seconds to state any idea, fact, or concept from the lesson, or to pass.

STEP 5: The ball is then passed to a new student, who must add more information to what was said or add new information (see the example below).

STEP 6: If a student cannot contribute, then he or she must pass the ball to someone who has not yet spoken; the next time this happens, the student must take a seat.

STEP 7: The game continues until only a few students are left standing. At that point, if the topic has been fully explored, the game may end. If you feel that the topic needs further exploration, allow the seated students to rejoin the game and add more information.

Example

Topic: The Age of Exploration

Teacher: The topic is the Age of Exploration. Javier. (tosses ball to Javier)

Javier: Europeans explored for riches. Emma. (tosses ball to Emma)

Emma: The Vikings explored to find new land. Padma. (tosses ball to Padma)

Padma: Many explorers tried to find a route to India to get spices. Max. (tosses ball to Max)

SHAPE-IT-UP SUMMARY

Purpose

The Shape-It-Up Summary strengthens and deepens understanding of major concepts for all students.

Why It Works

Students who prefer learning visually will excel using the Shape-It-Up Summary because this strategy puts information into a graphic organizer that helps them process and retain it.

ASSESSMENT OPTION

Formative Assessment

During the unit or at the close of a lesson, you can use the Shape-It-Up Summary reproducible to check where students are in their understanding of new information or a new concept. The checklist below will help you determine if students are ready to move on to the next stage in the learning. You can also use this summarizer to differentiate by product. In the square, have students write two concepts instead of four; in the triangle, have them write two important facts instead of three.

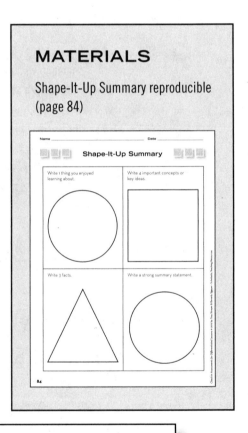

MATERIALS

Shape-It-Up Summary reproducible (page 84)

Shape-It-Up Summary Checklist

The first circle contains one item.	1 point
The square has four important concepts from the lesson.	4 points
The triangle has three accurate facts.	3 points
The second circle has a complete, well-written statement.	2 points

Check-in Assessments for Differentiated Lessons © 2012 by Troy Strayer & Beverly Strayer • Scholastic Teaching Resources

Sequence

STEP 1: Give a copy of the Shape-It-Up Summary reproducible to each student.

STEP 2: In the top left circle, have students write one thing that they enjoyed learning about during the lesson.

STEP 3: In the square, have students write four important concepts or key ideas they learned from the lesson. One concept should be written in each corner of the square.

STEP 4: In the triangle, have students write the three most important facts they learned from the lesson. One fact should be written in each corner of the triangle.

STEP 5: In the bottom right circle, have students write one statement that summarizes all the important concepts and facts they learned from the lesson. You may have to model this step a few times so students understand how to write a strong statement summary.

Shape-It-Up Summary

Write 1 thing you enjoyed learning about.

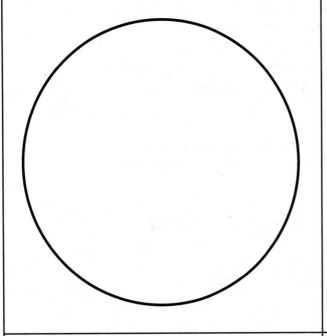

Write 4 important concepts or key ideas.

Write 3 facts.

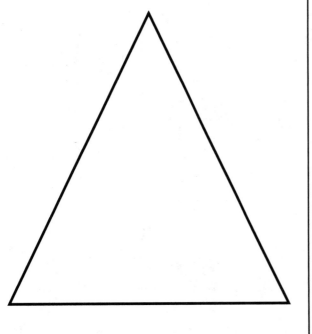

Write a strong summary statement.

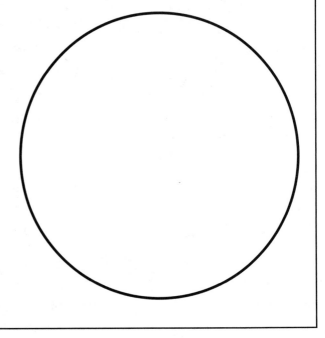

Check-in Assessments for Differentiated Lessons © 2012 by Troy Strayer & Beverly Strayer • Scholastic Teaching Resources

INCREDIBLE SHRINKING SUMMARY

Purpose

The Incredible Shrinking Summary strategy teaches students to summarize their learning in a clear, concise manner.

Why It Works

This summarizer allows students to "dump" all the information they have onto a page. As they write everything they know and reduce it to only the important details and concepts, they work through a streamlining process that allows them to further internalize the topic. This results in a concise, well-written summary.

ASSESSMENT OPTION

Formative Assessment

At the end of a lesson or unit, you can use the Incredible Shrinking Summary strategy to check where students are in their understanding of the information. If some students have difficulty "shrinking" the information, you may differentiate your instruction by allowing them to end their summaries after writing on the medium sticky note.

MATERIALS

3-inch by 5-inch index card; 2 sticky notes (one medium: 3-in. x 3-in., one small: 2-in. x 2-in.) for each student; pens or pencils

Sequence

☑ **STEP 1:** Share the topic(s) for the Incredible Shrinking Summary activity with students.

☑ **STEP 2:** Give each student an index card. Instruct students to write a summary of the topic on the index card.

☑ **STEP 3:** Then distribute a medium sticky note to each student. Tell them to revise the summary on the index card so it fits on the sticky note.

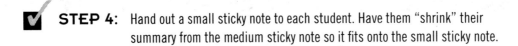

✔ **STEP 4:** Hand out a small sticky note to each student. Have them "shrink" their summary from the medium sticky note so it fits onto the small sticky note.

✔ **STEP 5:** Collect all three summaries—index card, medium sticky note, and small sticky note. Read a few of the shrinking summaries aloud. (See the example below.) This reflection and discussion provides time to clear up any misconceptions or to reinforce the content one more time. The discussion also models the correct way to do the Incredible Shrinking Summary for those who had difficulty in eliminating nonessential information.

Example

Topic: Main Character

INDEX CARD SUMMARY

> The most important character in a story is called the main character. When I write about main characters, I have to include dialogue, emotions, and exciting physical descriptions. A main character has to have a problem to solve in a narrative story.

MEDIUM STICKY NOTE SUMMARY

> When I write about a main character, I include dialogue, emotions, and a good physical description. A main character also has to have a problem to solve.

SMALL STICKY NOTE SUMMARY

> A vivid main character has emotions and talks to others. Every main character should have a problem to solve.

THINKING OUTSIDE THE BOX

Purpose

The Thinking Outside the Box summarizing strategy reinforces students' understanding of major concepts by having them make unique comparisons.

Why It Works

This activity helps students think creatively and deepen their understanding. It stretches their thinking to the synthesis level of Bloom's Taxonomy because they have to take a familiar concept and compare it with something out of the ordinary or totally unlike the concept.

ASSESSMENT OPTION

Formative Assessment

As you circulate, look for unusual comparisons that students make. Their explanations for doing so can give you valuable information about their grasp of concepts and information. You can gain critical information from the depth of each explanation of the comparisons. If you pair students by ability level to differentiate, they can help each other stretch their thinking.

MATERIALS

Thinking Outside the Box reproducible (page 89), pens or pencils

Sequence

☑ **STEP 1:** Identify the major concept for students to use in their comparison. Write it in the center of the Thinking Outside the Box reproducible.

☑ **STEP 2:** Determine which items students will compare with the major concept. Write each item in a box surrounding the concept (see the examples on the next page).

STEP 3: Model how to complete a Thinking Outside the Box reproducible with the class.

STEP 4: Pair students and then pass out one partially completed Thinking Outside the Box reproducible to each pair. (Because this strategy involves higher-level thinking, try this in pairs the first time. The next time, students should be able to complete the reproducible individually.)

STEP 5: Ask pairs to complete the reproducible. Then have them form a square with another pair and share their results. After they have had an opportunity to share, have each group of four choose one Thinking Outside the Box summary to share with the class.

Examples

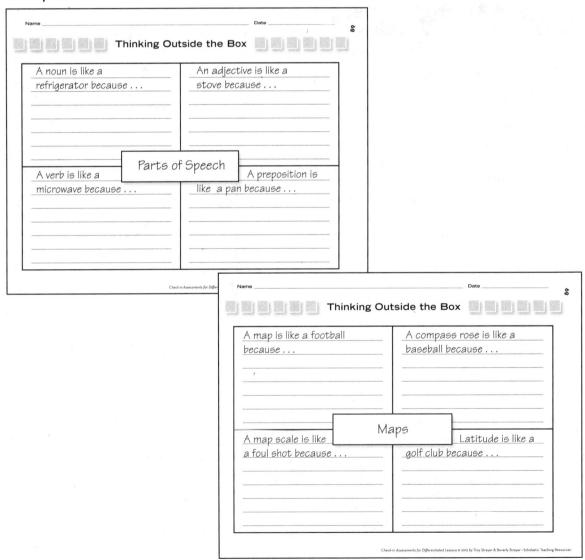

Thinking Outside the Box

Check-in Assessments for Differentiated Lessons © 2012 by Troy Strayer & Beverly Strayer • Scholastic Teaching Resources

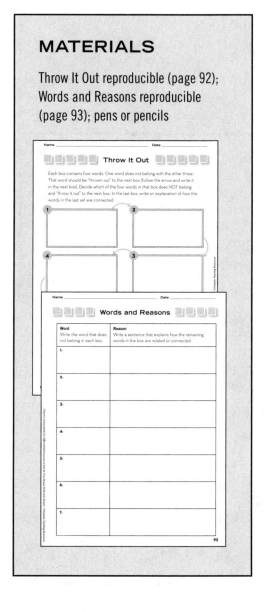

THROW IT OUT

Purpose

The Throw It Out strategy is an efficient way to summarize/review vocabulary before a unit test or state assessment in math, science, or social studies.

Why It Works

This strategy requires students to use the higher-level thinking skills of categorizing and classifying, which supports and increases understanding of key vocabulary words.

ASSESSMENT OPTION

Formative Assessment

At the close of a unit or the end of a lesson, you can use Throw It Out to check where students are in their understanding of the vocabulary. You can use the strategy as a graded assignment by assessing the choices students make using the strategy and their explanations of why they make those choices.

Sequence

✓ **STEP 1:** Adapt the Throw It Out reproducible for your lesson and make a copy for each student. Also create a sample reproducible with different information to use as a model.

✓ **STEP 2:** Using an overhead or a document camera, model how to complete the sample Throw It Out reproducible and the Words and Reasons reproducible to summarize the lesson. For instance, in the example on the next page, the word *variables* does not belong in box 1.

MATERIALS

Throw It Out reproducible (page 92); Words and Reasons reproducible (page 93); pens or pencils

Check-in Assessments for Differentiated Lessons © 2012 by Troy Strayer & Beverly Strayer • Scholastic Teaching Resources

Cross it out. Then write *variables* on the top line in box 2. Follow the arrows and repeat the process for each box. Write a sentence to show how the words in the last box, box 7, are related. As you "bump" each word, record it on the Words and Reasons reproducible and think aloud as you explain how the remaining words are related; for example, "You use prime numbers and composite numbers in prime factorization."

☑ STEP 3: Give a copy of the reproducibles to each student.

☑ STEP 4: Have them complete the reproducibles to summarize their learning.

Example: Math

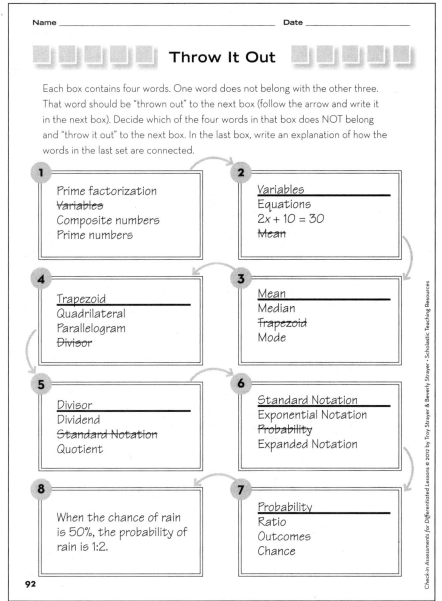

Name _____ Date _____

Throw It Out

Each box contains four words. One word does not belong with the other three. That word should be "thrown out" to the next box (follow the arrow and write it in the next box). Decide which of the four words in that box does NOT belong and "throw it out" to the next box. In the last box, write an explanation of how the words in the last set are connected.

1
Prime factorization
~~Variables~~
Composite numbers
Prime numbers

2
Variables
Equations
$2x + 10 = 30$
~~Mean~~

4
Trapezoid
Quadrilateral
Parallelogram
~~Divisor~~

3
Mean
Median
~~Trapezoid~~
Mode

5
Divisor
Dividend
~~Standard Notation~~
Quotient

6
Standard Notation
Exponential Notation
~~Probability~~
Expanded Notation

8
When the chance of rain is 50%, the probability of rain is 1:2.

7
Probability
Ratio
Outcomes
Chance

92

Check-in Assessments for Differentiated Lessons © 2012 by Troy Strayer & Beverly Strayer · Scholastic Teaching Resources

Throw It Out

Each box contains four words. One word does not belong with the other three. That word should be "thrown out" to the next box (follow the arrow and write it in the next box). Decide which of the four words in that box does NOT belong and "throw it out" to the next box. In the last box, write an explanation of how the words in the last set are connected.

1

2

4

3

5

6

8

7

Check-in Assessments for Differentiated Lessons © 2012 by Troy Strayer & Beverly Strayer • Scholastic Teaching Resources

 # Words and Reasons

Word Write the word that does not belong in each box.	Reason Write a sentence that explains how the remaining words in the box are related or connected.
1.	
2.	
3.	
4.	
5.	
6.	
7.	

Check-in Assessments for Differentiated Lessons © 2012 by Troy Strayer & Beverly Strayer • Scholastic Teaching Resources

YOU'VE GOT MAIL

Purpose

The You've Got Mail strategy gives students the opportunity to be part of every facet of a summary.

Why It Works

Many students do better when they work in groups rather than independently. This strategy is a cooperative learning activity, but it also has individual accountability.

ASSESSMENT OPTIONS

MATERIALS

one 3-inch by 5-inch index card and a sticky note for each student, pens or pencils

Formative Assessment

During a unit of study or at the end of a lesson, you can use the You've Got Mail strategy to check students' comprehension of information or a new concept. As students share answers to questions, they gain a different perspective on concepts and topics, which expands their knowledge.

Summative Assessment

To use this strategy as a prelude to a summative assessment, collect the cards and select a few questions or problems for it. Students love seeing their own questions on a test or quiz.

Sequence

☑ **STEP 1:** Put students in collaborative groups of four or five. Pass out one index card and a sticky note to each student.

☑ **STEP 2:** Explain that a thick question is one that cannot be answered "yes" or "no" and give a few examples.

☑ **STEP 3:** Have each group member write a problem or a review question that relates to the lesson or unit on the index card. Emphasize that the questions must be thick questions. Encourage students to ask questions that can be verified by looking through their notes or the text. (See the examples on the next page.)

☑ **STEP 4:** Tell each student to write the answer to his or her problem or question on the back of the index card.

☑ **STEP 5:** Ask groups to exchange their stack of problem or question cards.

☑ **STEP 6:** Have a student in each group read the first problem or question. The group then tries to solve or answer it. When the group members reach a consensus, they turn the card over to see if their response matches.

☑ **STEP 7:** If the answer does not match, the group writes its solution or answer on a sticky note, citing evidence from their notes or the text, and attaches it to the card.

☑ **STEP 8:** Tell groups to repeat the process until they have responded to each card.

☑ **STEP 9:** Have students return the cards to the original group. With the class, discuss and clarify any alternate responses attached to the index cards.

Example: Social Studies

What was the purpose of the Underground Railroad?	The abolitionists' purpose was to help slaves find paths to safety in free states or Canada.
(front)	(back)

Examples

Topic: SOCIAL STUDIES: UNDERGROUND RAILROAD

What was the purpose of the Underground Railroad?

Who were a few of the conductors on the Underground Railroad?

How were the Quakers involved in the Underground Railroad?

Who was Harriet Tubman?

Topic: HEALTH: BODY SYSTEMS

What does the skeletal system do for us?

Explain the blood's path through our body.

Explain the different types of muscle tissue.

What is the function of the nervous system?

How do the body systems work together to keep us alive?

Topic: MATH: MULTIPLICATION

What is 278 x 46?

What is 79 x 356?

What is 974 x 68?

What is 713 x 639?

Check-in Assessments for Differentiated Lessons © 2012 by Troy Strayer & Beverly Strayer • Scholastic Teaching Resources